CUSTOMER
EXPERIENCE2

**24 international CX professionals
share their current best-thinking
on achieving impact and visibility
through world-class best-practice CX**

W&M

Customer Experience 2

Edited by Naeem Arif, Ian Golding, Andrew Priestley

First published in July 2020

© W&M Publishing

www.writingmatterspublishing.com

ISBN 978-1-912774-65-4 (Pbk)

ISBN 978-1-912774-64-7 (eBk)

The rights of Naeem Arif (Editor), Ian Golding (Editor), Greg Melia, Marleen van Wijk, Sirte Pihlaja, Stefan Osthaus, Daniel Hoff-Rodrigues, Gayana Helder, Olga Guseva, Ruth Crowley, Spiros Milonas, Olga Potaptseva, Nick Lygo-Baker, Richard Jordan, Stacy Sherman, Bruno Guimarães, Betül Yılmaz, Michelle Badenhorst, Patricia Sanchez Diaz, Alec Dalton, Janelle Mansfield, Christopher Brooks, Hannah Foley, Umer Asif, Sarb Rana, Sharon Boyd, and Katie Stabler to be identified as contributing editors/authors of this work have been asserted in accordance with Sections 77 and 78 of the Copyright Designs and Patents Act, 1988.

A CIP catalogue record for this book is available from the British Library.

Disclaimer: *Customer Experience 2* is intended for information and education purposes only. This book does not constitute specific advice unique to your situation.

The views and opinions expressed in this book are those of the authors and do not reflect those of the Publisher and Resellers, who accept no responsibility for loss, damage or injury to persons or their belongings as a direct or indirect result of reading this book.

All people mentioned in case studies have been used with permission, and/or have had names, genders, industries and personal details altered to protect client confidentiality. Any resemblance to persons living or dead is purely coincidental.

To the best of our knowledge, the Publisher and Authors have complied with fair usage. The Publisher will be glad to rectify all future editions if omissions are bought to their attention.

Contents

Foreword - Greg Melia CEO CXPA

One can hardly surf the internet, read news, or watch entertainment these days without encountering a mention of Customer Experience (CX) – not surprising given the 165 million Google search results on the topic.

In April, a popular US television comedy series even offered a lead character a Director of Customer Experience position! In the professional sphere, we have seen similar growth, as evidenced by the 250% increase in the Customer Experience Professionals Association's LinkedIn followers - from 14,000 in August 2018 to over 36,000 today. While it is excellent that there is increased interest, it also creates new questions: What is CX and what is not? What are proven, real-world CX practices? How is CX similar and different throughout the world? What is needed next to advance the practice of CX?

In *Customer Experience 2*, we get to hear directly from individuals who have led CX initiatives and delivered better customer experiences. The authors of this book are a distinguished and diverse group, representing a wide range of industries, nations, and market strategies. Many hold the Certified Customer Experience Professional credential, the independent professional certification for CX professionals.

The book is organised based on the consensus driven CXPA CX competency framework.

You can trust that *Customer Experience 2* is built on a solid foundation, with accomplished guides who have met the professional standards for the practice of CX.

There has never been a more important time for a book like *Customer Experience 2*. The global impacts of COVID-19 challenge every business to focus on what's most important – building and maintaining a positive customer relationship. It's never been more critical to have and hone the four key interrelated elements essential to CX success: a culture of customer centricity, holistic alignment of systems and structures, clear connection to positive business performance outcomes, and the evolution of business practices through a focus on customer needs. The authors present authentic voices and perspectives based in practical CX experience, unhindered by exclusive proprietary methodologies or software.

We must foster the type of thinking reflected in *Customer Experience 2* to solidify the current practice of CX and define what comes next. If these commitments ring true to you, you are in for a treat — and I encourage you to further the CX movement at *www.cxpa.org*.

Together in Advancing CX,

Greg Melia, CAE

CEO Customer Experience Professionals Association (CXPA)

Welcome To Customer Experience 2

If you Google Customer Experience or CX, you will get over 4 billion hits, which will include a series of blogs, videos, case studies and definitions. Although the importance of CX is increasing every day, it is not something new and brands have been using this as a strategy since time began, they just didn't attribute it to the CX concepts.

So why is this so important at this time?

We live in an age of personalisation, businesses should focus on being unique. Whilst SEO and big data are important, they won't replace a friendly welcome and personal attention. At this time, excellent customer service is how businesses are dominating the marketplace; customers will remember your service much longer than your price.

I am a big advocate of putting the Customer First in everything you do, as repeat customers are way more profitable than new customers. This is not something that can only be learned in an MBA and this is certainly not something that belongs to the selected few influencers who have an audience. This is something that we see every day around the world and in this series of books, we share the best thinking and experience from those people who are at the customer facing end.

In this series of books and podcasts, our aim is to give a platform to those innovators who are doing great things in the CX field to share their knowledge and experience to the rest of the world.

The more we share, the more we learn. Who wins? As we push the boundaries, ultimately the customer wins and I guess that's what we are aiming for, to deliver better experiences.

If you are reading this book and have a case study to share, we want to hear about it for our upcoming projects. In the first instance, you can reach out to me and I will try and connect your story to an audience.

Naeem Arif

Naeem has three decades of experience as a retail business owner and CX consultant with specific expertise in the customer retention functions. During his time he has had the opportunity to work with senior leaders and is known for 'putting the customer first' into every solution he designs.

As well as writing several books, he is the founder of the Customer Experience series and can be contacted through the following social channels.

Naeem@NAConsulting.co.uk

Twitter / @NAConsultingLtd

Linkedin / NaeemArif

Facebook / NAConsultingLtd

1. Customer Centric Culture

The right mindset, attitude and commitment

Ten Things About Customer Experience I Wish I'd Known Earlier

Marleen van Wijk

When I started my first job in Customer Experience (CX) I had little experience in this area. My boundless naïveté helped me in accepting challenges that were far outside my comfort zone. I never realized the difficulty of the challenges ahead of me. Maybe this was for the best. I learned CX the hard way: by trial and error, by making mistakes and turning them into best practices. It made me constantly fall back on my skills, instinct, enthusiasm, and strong belief in a better world for customers.

If I knew then what I know now, I, for sure, would have approached many situations differently. In this article I share with you the ten things about CX that I wish I would have known earlier. Read and apply these points and I promise you that your CX journey will kickstart into high gear. Knowing the secret ingredients beforehand will help you to oversee what is coming and prevent you from making the same mistakes I did. Being aware of the following points will help you to make CX work faster and enjoy greater success.

So, here we go.

1. There Is No End To CX
It Is An Infinite Way Of Running Your Organisation

I am impatient by nature. I prefer to move fast on projects that have a clear beginning and end. This is a rhythm that I feel comfortable with. Unfortunately for me, CX does not work like that. Customers have been around forever and without them you are out of business. So technically, customers are always there, so there cannot be a start and an end date.

Neither is CX to be considered a project. In a project, different activities are undertaken to create new products and services. CX could consist of different short-term projects but generally consists of a much broader scope.

For me, CX is a state of mind and a way to run your organisation. It demands long-term work and short-term milestones. If you see CX through 'short-term glasses', it will not work. CX is about anticipating customer behaviours and identifying ways to improve your customer journeys. This can never be short-term since customer needs are always changing. If you consider CX to have a finish line, you will not adapt to these evolving needs. You need to have a long-term focus and commitment to create an environment of continuous improvement. Do share a variety of shorter-term results if you want to keep your senior management on board. Showing milestones and celebrating success will help you to drive engagement in this endless CX journey without a final destination.

2. You Cannot Create Outstanding Customer Experiences
Just By Yourself

CX management is about constantly working on creating amazing end-to-end customer journeys. This cannot be done just by you. In order to improve, you will need cross-functional expertise, involvement and commitment from employees across the organisation. Everyone in the organisation plays an important role, not only in designing these experiences but also in delivering them. It is only human that when behaviour is expected from you later, you need to be engaged from the start.

Make sure your focus is not only with customer-facing employees - do not forget about your mid- and back office colleagues. So even though they do not have day-to-day customer contact, they still are an important part of the chain. Also, by involving them, no one feels left out.

For me personally it is very tempting to sometimes not involve everyone, as the work is done quicker and results are provided faster. But the truth is that CX is something you cannot do on your own. CX is a shared responsibility and concerns all of us. Ideas or strategies that were created too fast and in isolation will not fly for long, or at all.

Without the input and engagement of all layers of the organisation, CX will remain ad hoc and will never become seamless and intentional.

3. Executive Buy-In Is Vital To Succeed

Over the years, I have learned that true CX transformation demands the commitment of the highest executives in an organisation. CX should be on their radar. You can maybe start off without it, but at some point in the journey, management buy-in and active top management involvement, will be crucial.

Implementing CX impacts every single individual in a company and can therefore be seen as a cultural transformation. Successful cultural changes always start; and must be driven from the top to make sure all individuals are on board. The executives need to get all organisational levels aligned for each ancillary step in the customer journey. By doing this it becomes part of the culture from the top level all the way down to the employees in the "most invisible" layers of the journey. The executive commitment will help to drive the improvement of experiences at the working level.

I dare say that without buy-in of at least one board member, you might as well better stop right now: you are wasting your time. If you feel there is a lack of leadership buy-in, take the bull by the horns and openly discuss your concerns. It is your task as a CX professional to hold the mirror up. Make them aware of what sort of behaviour is needed to drive this transformation. Prevent passive executive support since this will influence everyone and will affect and slow down your hard work. Without the prioritisation, fast tracking and long-haul commitment at executive level for CX as a topic, the implementation will fail. You will be constantly swimming against the tide.

4. Make Sure You And Your Stakeholders Speak The Same Language

The term Customer Experience has gained a lot of traction in last decade. CX is everywhere. When you browse the Internet, you will find that there are many definitions out there. As a result, people have different interpretations of what CX is. Some will say it is the new marketing, others will relate to it in a more digital way. Quite often CX and customer centricity are used interchangeably.

Like I have said, CX concerns all of us and it is therefore desirable that you need your stakeholders to be on the same page regarding definitions. When they are not, you could find yourself working twice as hard to achieve your goals, without any guarantee of succeeding. It could also lead to miscommunication followed by confusion. To successfully work together on CX in the coming years, you need to speak the same language. Investing in this at an early stage, will save you discussion and time at the end.

Although desirable, it can be quite a challenge to achieve this, especially in large companies. My advice is to start small and work from there. Decide on the message you would like to get across. Start with sharing this with your own team followed by the executives. From there work towards the rest of the organisation step-by-step. Keep it simple at all times. Your message should be comprehensible for everyone from a senior manager to a person cleaning the office.

5. Do Not Assume, Act Upon Facts

It surprised me how often employees, when improving customer experiences, make assumptions on what customers want. There is a logical explanation here.

When people work in a company for many years, and have lots of experience, so it is only natural that they will have an opinion on what is best for customers. However, customer behaviour changes constantly. We cannot simply rely on what we have learned or seen work in the past. In order to improve we need to invest in understanding the constantly changing customer's needs. We should therefore never assume but always measure and check.

This is where the importance of the voice of the customer and the measurement comes in. Please always ask, validate, test and co-create instead of creating things by yourself. Act upon facts. Facts that expose customer drivers and uncover the in-the-moment customer requirements. And do this on a continuous base, never stop asking for input and feedback. At the end it is about the customer and not about you, no matter how well intended your efforts are.

6. Always Use A Framework

Imagine solving a 1000 pieces jigsaw without starting with the border. You will manage, I am sure, but it is tough. Things in general go faster when you have a framework. A shared structure to work from that helps in how to approach a challenge.

Same goes for CX. Without a doubt, in your organisation there are already many great customer related initiatives. Why not bring all these initiatives together into one integrated approach. It will help you to keep a helicopter view; to have better focus; to improve faster and guide your organisation towards success. I can assure you the whole thing will fall together.

Whatever framework you will choose, make sure that it is 'simple' - so straightforward that every employee in your organisation is able to understand, remember and use it. Diving into too much detail is not always necessary and will only slow you down. A good framework always includes strategy, measurement, improvement and culture.

7. Always Be Ready To 'Talk CX'

CX requires long-term work and short-term profiling. Therefore, it is important to 'talk CX' constantly, anytime, anywhere. Good communication plays a vital role here.

What I advise you to do is to constantly inform your stakeholders about short-term achievements. Keep mentioning why you do what you do, what the next level looks like and how you will get there. And that you can't do this alone. Keep everyone's eye on this prize constantly and remind them of the importance of their involvement. It will take time to show the effect and you do not want to lose them along the way.

Next to standing in front of a group of people with a beamer and perfectly prepared slide deck, always be ready for a CX chit-chat. These spontaneous talks happen more often and out of the blue than you might think. A quick chat in the elevator, while waiting in line to get your morning coffee or after parking your car in the garage. These moments are all opportunities to profile your plans. Networking is key.

8. CX Is An Intangible Discipline Full Of Contrast

Prepare yourself for a discipline full of contrast. I will give you some examples.

First of all, CX is strategic: it needs a plan. Executive buy-in is key.

Simultaneously, you cannot do without the engagement of the people at the floor. It concerns what is decided in the board but directly impacts the ones that have customer contact. So, at the same time CX is very operational. It should be ready for use and very pragmatic.

CX can also be very complex. It concerns alignment between channels, processes, touch points, journeys, IT systems and people. Like any other cultural change or attempt to change behaviour, a CX transition requires hard work, focus and time. From customer research you will find many possibilities for improvement. You will often find yourself in a situation where you will feel overwhelmed and you do not know where to start. Contrariwise, CX at its root it is quite simple. The differences are in the little things and can be done by a single individual. Like a proactive support call or a handwritten thank you note. Also, with the right priority setting based upon customer, employee and business' needs, you will know the expected impact and what to work on first.

CX covers many facets. It is everything and everything in between and can therefore feel very intangible but in exchange I will promise you it will never be boring.

9. You Cannot Rush Transformation

On average implementing a CX framework takes between six to eight years. Assuming there are no important organisational changes like new leadership or restructuring of the company. Sometimes when there is an urgency, companies try to accelerate.

I have to disappoint you. There are no possible shortcuts. You simply can't rush transformation. It is straightforward. All good things take time: beautiful gardens, tasty fruit, Italian risotto and so too for customer loyalty.

You cannot afford to cut corners. More haste, less speed. Like I said, this is long term work and in order to have success, it is critical to operate at the pace of what your organisation can accommodate. If you speed up the pace of transformation, this could be damaging

10. CX Is An Effortful But Worthwhile Journey

I am not going to lie to you. Successful CX can feel like driving on a very bumpy road. It takes focus, time and is hard work. I do not want to sound negative here, but I also do not want you to be blindsided about the years ahead of you. CX requires persistence, patience, a positive attitude, people skills, practical experience, persuasiveness and collaboration with different teams and levels in the organisation. Try to enjoy the ride, you will see beautiful scenery along the way. If you can enjoy these small things you will find it was very much worth it.

Working in CX has learned and given me so much. No, it was not always easy but remember that every single day you are working to make the world a better one for both your customers and your coworkers. With that in mind you can cope with resistance and challenges along the way. Keep your eyes on the prize, every time you feel the world is against you. Be prepared for everything. I know now what I, by instinct, knew back then - never ever give up because organisations and attitudes can and will change!

About Marleen van Wijk

With 17.5 years of international experience in customer experience, marketing and manager roles, Marleen van Wijk, CCXP, helps companies to build, improve and drive customer strategies.

As managing director of NeCXus, a customer experience management consultancy and training firm, she currently helps companies to better connect to customers by using an integrated approach that is based on years of practical experience. Besides giving CX Masterclasses in the Benelux, Marleen currently accompanies companies in the travel, logistics and banking industry in their Customer Experience transformations.

Marleen is a passionate CX believer, an energetic trainer and communicator, hands-on and challenging organisations to create a fact-based customer centric culture.

Marleen previously worked for Canon Europe, KPN -the largest telecom in The Netherlands-, market research agency Ipsos and PostNL.

www.necxus.agency

https://www.linkedin.com/in/marleenvanwijk

Customer Experience 2

Get Ready... Get Serious... PLAY!

Sirte Pihlaja

"You can discover more about a person in an hour of play than a year of conversation."

- Plato, Athenian philosopher

In this chapter, I will share with you how using LEGO® bricks can unlock and encourage creativity in our co-workers to deliver a great result for both our employees and our customers.

George Land developed a creativity test to help select innovative engineers and scientists for NASA in 1965. When, three years later, he applied this test to a group of children, he could not fathom the results. Out of the 1,600 children between the ages of 4 and 5 selected for his study, 98% scored a creative genius level. The same children were tested again at the age of 10, with only 30% scoring this level. Five years later, only 12% were deemed measurably creative.

The same test has been applied to over 1 million adults, and only 2% have scored at the genius level. What is going on here? Land concluded that we learn non-creative behaviour as we progress through our education. As we are taught convergent thinking, our divergent thinking - CREATIVITY - is drained from us. (Land, G. & Jarman, B. 1998)

Children are naturally geared toward being creative and non-judgmental. But if creativity is not something we learn, but rather unlearn, what can we do to be at our creative best to keep up with Tech Giants such as Facebook, Amazon, Apple, Netflix and Google (FAANG)? Or the likes of AirBnB, Disney and Zappos, who rule in People Experiences? Luckily, the 5-year-old creative genius in us never disappears completely. We just need to find a way to tap into this inner child to rediscover our true capabilities.

Children gain their cognitive skills - learning about themselves, other people, relationships, and communication - through play. Play is the most fundamental learning mechanism. It is also said that you learn better when you play because learning through play happens spontaneously. When we try out new things, we construct new knowledge effortlessly. And that, my friend, is precisely what you should be doing as a customer experience professional.

Take Your Business And Pleasure Seriously

Our societies are facing unprecedented challenges. We need to adapt, be creative, and come up with new solutions to these problems very quickly. We must understand our customers and employees to deliver what they need and want right now, to help sustain a healthy business. Play is an excellent vehicle for creating this understanding and coming up with innovative solutions.

"Take your pleasure seriously."

- Charles Eames, American industrial designer

Indeed, many management thinkers are now advocating that businesses should be more playful, to embrace the unknown and innovate. They feel it's the only way to keep up with the competition.

More play can bring about a new wave of valuing other people, relationships, and supporting each other in business. It leads to lower levels of stress, healthier personnel, and more engaged employees - all signs of a forward-looking company. All of these positive effects, in turn, are bound to propel your business growth, profits, and success.

I believe that people in general - and employees in particular - need to be HAPPY, so they care about delivering happiness to others. Without happy employees, you cannot have great customer experiences. It's that simple.

Play is often associated with happiness and joy, having fun. A pioneer of the scientific study of happiness, Mihaly Csikszentmihalyi insists that happiness is not something that "just happens".

"It is not enough to be happy to have an excellent life.
The point is to be happy while doing things that stretch our skills,
that help us grow and fulfil our potential."
- Mihaly Csikszentmihalyi, Hungarian-American psychologist

Csikszentmihalyi coined the term "flow" to depict a state of pure satisfaction, where you find yourself fully immersed in doing something that requires your creative capabilities. It takes significant preparation and planning, all the while setting suitably demanding challenges to oneself and others.

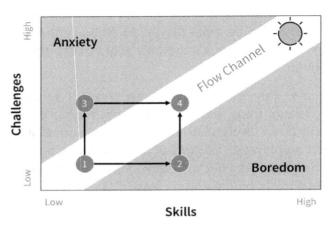

Picture 1. According to Csikszentmihalyi, the ideal place to be is in the "Flow Channel", where the challenge of what you're doing is roughly equal to the skills you have to do that. The activities that you are motivated to get done let you experience flow and are the ones that will make you the happiest. (Bailey, C. 2013)

Creativity Is A Critical Capability

Play is not the opposite of work - boredom is. In fact, work benefits from play. Stuart Brown, a psychiatrist, MD, and a leading authority on Play, goes as far as saying that play is like oxygen as it "goes mostly unnoticed or unappreciated until it is missing". (Brown, S. 2009)

Creative thinking is a critical capability that we need to find within ourselves to adapt, solve problems and innovate. Stuart Brown believes that having a playful atmosphere not only attracts young talent but play at work boosts creativity and productivity in people of all ages. According to Brown, when we make learning a fun activity, employees will learn better as well as be far more likely to use their new skills.

You might believe we are either "born creative", or we are not. But that's a myth! It causes many of us to be uncertain of our ability to be creative and afraid to fail.

A playful organisation has happy, motivated, and committed employees. They are inspired and have fun together, all the while performing better. In a business that has instilled play, people are allowed to experiment and take creative risks. When it is ok to fail, the whole organisation learns and succeeds faster. By welcoming failure, your company culture matures.

Build A Playful Culture For Your Employees

Play helps us connect with the people around us. At work, this means that even the most introverted among us find it easier to approach others through shared play. They may also find commonalities with their peers by revealing a little bit more about themselves.

Common goals and objectives set by the rules of organised play help teams become more aligned and united. With an increased sense of belonging, the team grows stronger and closer together, and conflicts get resolved swiftly.

Instead of a depressed and stressed workforce - a prime reason for lost productivity - organisations can enjoy workers who find their "flow" effortlessly. In a company culture that advocates play, people feel refreshed and energised, and learning and creativity get a boost.

When The Play Gets Serious - Case LEGO®

Play has an essential role in business, as it puts you in the right mindset and allows you space to think differently and - you guessed it - unlocks your CREATIVITY. The need to introduce more creativity in an organisation is vital to its well-being.

But what if your company does not want or cannot afford to invest in renovating the business premises by installing slides and playgrounds to build a "creative environment" in the footsteps of the giants? What if you, instead, prefer to play it "seriously"? Rest assured, play is not just about external facilities, it can - and it should be to a high degree - about the ways of working. So, the only investment you need to make may very well be between your ears and with your own hands.

How do you ingrain play into your working habits? Enter LEGO® SERIOUS PLAY® (LSP). A methodology created by LEGO® for themselves in the mid-1990s as they were on the lookout for better ways to reinvent themselves.

LSP was the brainwork of two academic professors, Johan Roos and Bart Victor. Whilst founded on a sound theoretical background, LSP is as practical a tool as they come and an extraordinary catalyst for change.

The methodology revolves around challenges set by the facilitator and the models that participants build out of LEGO® bricks. But LSP is not about playing with bricks, nor is it team building. It is something much bigger! Something which provides the platform needed to give everyone the equal footing to be heard as the company creates its future business and culture through story-telling and metaphors.

LEGO® assembled a line of "serious" bricks to help construct and play business scenarios out, make critical business decisions and bring valuable results to organisations. LEGO® SERIOUS PLAY® truly gives your brain a hand. As a tactile experience, it immerses the players into a state of flow.

Business development	Customer experience management	Employee experience & engagement
• Development of dynamic strategies and action plans	• CX strategy work and action plans	• Developing EX strategy and action plans
• Development of strategic preparedness/ thinking	• Developing strategies on different levels of the organisation	• Reviewing current EX strategy
• Development and release of innovative potential	• Defining customer needs/building empathy	• Defining employee needs/building empathy
• Solving very complex and/or conflicting strategic, managerial and organisational challenges/changes	• Exploring the audience or market of an organisation or program	• Building identity
• Organisational development	• Creating a landscape of existing target groups and potential new ones	• Analyzing and solving problems within an organization
• Mapping of core identity, core tasks and core processes	• Attracting new audiences in the target market	• Kick-starting creative thinking
• Brand development	• Innovation	• Supporting team identity
• Project start-up	• Visualising theories or models	• Facilitating constructive dialogue
• Project intervention	• Solving very complex and/or conflicting challenges	• Creating a more cohesive team/unit structure
• Simulation of major changes and projects	• Simulation of major changes	• Exploring the identity of an organization or team/unit
• Optimisation of processes	• Optimisation of processes	• Developing a set of simple guiding principles
• Development of management teams	• Development of (management) teams	• Guidelines for benefiting from digitalisation/transformation
• Development of teams in general	• Employee development	
• Employee development	• Development of shared ownership, culture and values	
	• Iteration of ideas *before* and *after* implementation and delivery	
	• Testing prototypes as part of service design process	

Table 1. Examples of use areas for LEGO® SERIOUS PLAY® in business development, customer experience management and employee experience & engagement.

Better People Experiences One Brick At A Time

LEGO® SERIOUS PLAY® was created to reinvent the business and all of the original applications needed to support LEGO® in their endeavour. These applications range from defining your company purpose and real-time strategy work to building your culture (identity) at different levels of the organisation: leadership, divisions, business units and teams, or indeed at the individual employee level.

LEGO® also created an LSP application intended for use in times of significant change - not very much unlike the present circumstances. Organisations can use it when they face critical disruptions, such as digitalisation, for resolving conflicts and for mergers and acquisitions, when there is a need to get alignment on a strategic and cultural level (see Table 1, p29).

Since LEGO® released LSP as open-source in 2010, proficient LSP practitioners have come up with their applications in different domains. For example, Design Thinking and People Experiences development-related applications (CX Play) are helpful in strategy and brand work and creating better customer experiences (CX) and employee experiences (EX).

Summary

In CX and EX development, in particular, LSP can be used to create personas, plan and manage customer journeys, design experiences, employee engagement...even for CX strategies! It is a facilitation method unlike any other, which resonates with everyone and helps energise participants so they can get in the flow and be more creative. Building brick by brick with discussions running freely, people manage to get much deeper into the conversations. LSP fast-tracks your work and helps concretise ideas, even in prototyping.

"People tend to forget that play is serious."

- David Hockney, British contemporary artist

LSP is a very serious tool for facilitating change. It reignites our innate creativity and directs it to CX, EX and business development. It sets our minds free to construct new possibilities, instead of relying on having the "right answers" and merely replicating the past. Using creative and playful methodologies, such as LEGO® SERIOUS PLAY®, allows us to imagine and build a new future not only for our businesses but for the whole world! Wouldn't this be the perfect time for your organisation to try it out?

Playful business

Let people experiment

Attract the right talent

Yearn to make customers happy

Sources

- Bailey, C. (Sep 12, 2013). How to 'Flow': Here's the most magical chart you'll come across today. https://alifeofproductivity.com/how-to-experience-flow-magical-chart (accessed June 7th, 2020)

- Brown, S. (2009). Play: How it Shapes the Brain, Opens the Imagination, and Invigorates the Soul. Penguin Group.

- Brown, S. (May 2008). Play is more than just fun. TEDx speech from Serious Play 2008 Conference. https://www.ted.com/talks/stuart_brown_play_is_more_than_just_fun (accessed June 6th, 2020)

- Land, G. & Jarman, B. (1998.), Breakpoint and Beyond: Mastering the Future Today. Harper Collins Publishers, Inc.

- Land, G. (December 2011). The Failure Of Success. TEDx Tucson speech. https://youtu.be/ZfKMq-rYtnc (accessed June 6th, 2020)

- LEGO, the LEGO logo, SERIOUS PLAY, the Minifigure, the Brick and the Knob configuration are trademarks of the LEGO Group.

About Sirte Pihlaja

Sirte Pihlaja (Certified Customer Experience Professional, Trained Facilitator of LEGO® SERIOUS PLAY® Methods and Materials) is the CEO and Customer Experience Optimiser of Shirute, the first customer experience agency in Finland.

She heads the activities of the global Customer Experience Professionals Association (CXPA) in Finland, is one of the Association's Founding Members, and a member of its International Advisory Board. Sirte is an internationally known CX/EX expert, a coach, designer and strategist with over 25 years of experience in advising large international corporations and brands in different industries. Sirte is known for translating customer understanding to concrete actions and results in a fast and cost-efficient way. She is especially fond of creative methodologies and regularly plays with LEGO bricks with her clients.

To connect with Sirte or follow her on social media:

LinkedIn: www.linkedin.com/in/sirte

Twitter: @sirteace

Instagram: @sirteace

Facebook: www.facebook.com/shirute

Visit websites:

www.shirute.fi

www.cxplay.fi

www.shirute.fi/cem-benchmark

Coffee, Coins, And Happiness – Why Every CX Initiative Benefits From EX

Stefan Osthaus

Good experience initiatives often start with a great cup of coffee. Today, it will be you having a coffee with your head of HR! But let me start at the beginning!

Customer And Employee Satisfaction Are Two Sides Of The Same Coin!

What at first glance sounds like a calendar motto is one of the most important lessons I have learned in my career. Let me give you an example: In one of the largest Silicon Valley companies I was responsible for both Customer Experience (CX) and Employee Experience (EX) for many years. I was also responsible for customer service with over 6,500 employees in call centres around the world.

If you stumble across the term *call centre*, you're right: today we use more inspiring terms like service centres or similarly aspirational words ... but at the time, overseas centres were real *call centres – sweat shops* as they say.

Especially in the Indian centres, agents had to repeat every statement of our American customers. This "rephrasing" should avoid misunderstandings. In addition, detailed scripts were prescribed for the answers to ensure that the agents also responded politely and in conformity with the brand.

You are already guessing it: a conversation in which your counterpart repeats each of your statements and then answers by reading text templates can at best be described as robotic. The intended effect of softening the strong Indian accent for American customers through rephrasing and scripting backfired. Customers were confused at best, but often upset. The Indian colleagues – all excellently educated – were deeply frustrated. The average length of service in our teams was far less than a year – a monstrous effort for HR to constantly re-hire and train new employees!

At some point we realized what nonsense that was.

We abolished rephrasing and scripting – first for testing purposes, then very quickly indefinitely. Suddenly, highly motivated and well-trained young people could show what they were capable of. The result were profound, human, emphatic, and highly professional conversations that delighted our customers.

Customer satisfaction scores skyrocketed immediately. And also employee satisfaction rose sharply. Shortly afterwards, we found that the average length of service of agents increased, which made life much easier for HR and call centre management and resulted in significant cost savings.

What I learned then, a few years ago, is still true today: Customer satisfaction and employee satisfaction are two sides of the same coin!

How Can You Leverage EX For Your CX?

Don't assume that there is "just no time for EX" while focusing on CX! That would be like not wanting to pump up your flat tires before a scenic bike tour, just because you want to focus on pedalling – a big waste of energy!

Because just as inflated tires make cycling easier, motivated employees reduce the effort required for every CX initiative.

Imagine the difference: You stand in front of the assembled staff and make a fiery speech for more customer satisfaction and demand the support of all employees. Or – much better – you make the same fiery speech about how you want to have not only the most satisfied and loyal customers but also become the best place to work. Believe me: I have seen the spark ignite in the second scenario much more often than in the first!

For CX and EX initiatives, 1 + 1 = 3 actually applies! Both follow a very similar framework and share similar methods and tools. Both are initiatives, not temporary projects.

Let me share a few tips on how to pragmatically complement your CX with a focus on EX!

A Lot Works Just The Same: The Recipe For Great CX And EX

If you look at what makes your current CX initiative successful, then you find five things:

1. **A clear idea of your strategy** Which role should customer satisfaction play in your organisation?

2. **A culture that supports your strategy**
   Are your employees empowered to do what it takes?

3. **A solid organisational set-up for CX**
   Orchestrating your CX initiative matures from a somebody's hobby to a full-time leadership role with the right team

4. **Effective governance** The right attention for the initiative everywhere in your organisation

5. **Great data** analysed for profound insights leading to swift action

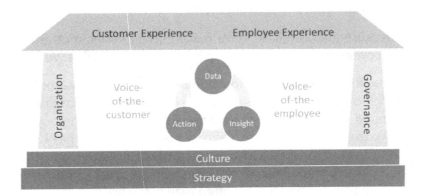

These success factors need to be built for your CX initiative – and, guess what, they will be what you need for a great EX initiative as well! The great news is: both initiatives will boost each other and be much more efficient together than each of them individually. Just like putting two appointments into one business trip – instead of just one.

Here's What You As A CX Leader Need To Know About EX

The right listening is the be-all and end-all of a great experience initiative! And right means with the right structure, the right methods, and the necessary endurance!

The difference in listening

As a CX practitioner you know the role of customer journey maps in CX. The employee experience in an organisation is usually not such a journey. I found that employees view their work more holistically than in a phase model. With my clients, for example, I always look at the four Ps: *pay* (all elements of the renumeration), *play* (the quality and convenience of the workplace), *productivity* (the ability to grow and work freely), and *purpose* (the match between company and individual values).

What remains the same in EX as in CX is that you measure employee sentiment at important touchpoints – and you better do so with more than the dreaded annual employee survey!

How to listen to employees

Before you create a single new survey, see what's already there that tells you about employee sentiment. Nobody likes an experience initiative that comes with loads of new surveys!

When I spend a few days with clients talking to the different teams like HR, facilities, or IT, I typically find 50-70 existing data sources for employee sentiment. They range from the rate at which higher positions are filled from within, the percentage of employees showing up for the holiday party, the responses to IT's ticket closing survey and much more. Often, this data sits in company silos without much attention being paid to it.

Our clients love our method where we pick the most relevant data sources and aggregate them into the Great People Index without much effort. This index is a perfect supplement to the existing annual employee surveys, as it provides a monthly snapshot of the employee sentiment.

The annual employee survey in companies is a much-hated tool. Weeks of preparation, pressure to participate, and time-consuming analysis that rarely leads to tangible results – the annual employee survey must be the most dreaded tool in the world of EX!

Plus, the Net Promoter Score (NPS), which is completely unsuitable for measuring employee sentiment, is often used as a measurement scale. I have often seen eNPS results fluctuate so much that everyone in the organisation was just plainly frustrated about meaningless results from the survey.

So instead, build on what's already there, and you will have an index that you can double-click on to see where issues arise. And then sit down with employees and have a personal, meaningful conversation in a group session or a handful of interviews to get to the root of the issue.

Get employee feedback with the right stamina

In addition to not pulling for too much feedback from employees via boring surveys, let them push it to you effectively. If your company suggestion system is rotting away with hardly any suggestions coming-in, then boost it to new life with the right incentives and communication impulses.

But don't stop there! If not in place already, design with your HR team an effective system of exit interviews with leaving employees. I have always found exit interviews with my employees a great source of insight delivering many ideas for how we could improve.

Good listening is simple; you can always just call together a round of employees and conduct a group interview when topics arise. Why is the new inner courtyard not used for breaks and collaboration? Why is the use of the canteen declining? What could a new version of supplementary voluntary insurance for employees look like? Such questions are ideal for involving employees early on by asking their wishes and opinions.

Data - Insight – Action:
Only Those Who Listen May Ask Questions!

As you build your EX initiative and start listening to the team, make sure nobody gets to ask questions who is not ready to react to what they hear. Collecting feedback and not doing anything with it is worse than not asking for feedback in the first place!

But once everyone in the organisation is eagerly awaiting the next index or the next round of feedback from teams and customers to swiftly turn them into improvement activities, then your goal is achieved! From here, everyone listens. All management levels and employees listen to what customers and employees have to say. From here, opportunities for continuous improvement are identified, prioritised, and implemented.

Now you have created the organisation that is permanently getting better based on feedback!

How To Blow-Up A Silo

As promising as combining CX and EX sounds, don't be disappointed if your head of HR is not 200% enthusiastic about this new idea of yours! HR teams in many large organisations are recovering only slowly from the cost-cutting madness of the turn of the millennium. The ruins of excessively melted down HR areas with globally consolidated service centres and a minimal number of HR employees on site are still smoking in many companies. But others have adapted to declining unemployment in many countries and the challenges of filling vacancies with the right candidates.

No matter your HR muscle, different from introducing a new ERP system (all or nothing!), an EX initiative can be launched and maintained on a shoestring if needed.

The recipe for success is as follows: The heads of the CX and HR departments meet to determine how much time and resources are realistically available for a joint optimisation of customer and employee satisfaction. Better start small and then increase over time rather than having to abandon an overly resource-intensive initiative.

Both then put together a pragmatic initiative with their teams and get started. However small the joint initiative may be, its objectives must be precisely defined to make success measurable. This success is the fuel that makes the initiative grow and gain momentum.

What's To Gain?

Most companies I work with describe themselves as customer oriented. Not quite as many – but more and more – realise how costly and difficult it is to replace a great employee who left.

But there is more to gain from great EX! Here are some of the key advantages you can enjoy when jointly optimising your CX and EX:

- Employees are more motivated to improve the customer experience if the initiative also delivers improvements for them.

- Team suggestions not only increase job satisfaction, but often also make products or processes better, faster, or cheaper.

- Better, faster, and cheaper products and processes improve your production cost, your service, your logistics – you name it! This gives you extra resources for quality, marketing, and customer service, which leads to ... you get the point, right?

- Happy employees are a pleasure to deal with – ask your customers!

- Being a great place to work will be noticed! You will be able to hire faster and with better quality. Teams will spend less time overworked because of unfilled vacancies, more happiness right there! And think about the better service levels for customers coming from that ...

You see, your efforts of combining CX and EX are creating a virtuous cycle, no matter how humble your initial initiative is. And now, call your head of HR and take them out for a coffee. You have a lot to talk about!

About Stefan Osthaus

Stefan has been a leader in Fortune 500 companies and an advisor to multinational organisations who seek to become more customer centric for more than 20 years. His passion and expertise have helped to improve the experiences of over half a billion customers and hundreds of thousands of employees around the globe. When he doesn't work with clients somewhere on  the planet, Stefan shares his insights and anecdotes as a global keynote speaker, trainer, and author.

Contacts and links

www.experience5.com

www.greatpeopleindex.com

linkedin.com/in/stefanosthaus

The Untold Recruitment Story - From Transactional To CX

Daniel Hoff-Rodrigues

The recruitment industry is notorious for its lack of customer experience. We talk about our story and how we have sought to change the opinions of the industry through the creation of {CX}^{2} Talent Solutions.

Recruitment is transactional and reactive in nature, a step-by-step process that culminates in using a candidate as a commodity. During nine years of working for different recruitment businesses this approach never changed, the goal remained a quick win using underhand tactics. In order to change an industry like recruitment, you need to prove the system and beliefs wrong and describe a new perspective and ideology.

For years we wanted to create a new type of recruitment business. We knew it was an overcrowded market, so we needed something that was different. For two years we planned and wrote and planned! Eventually we came up with a 22-page business plan, only one page of which was focused on financials and cash flow, the rest was our new approach.

Our idea was to support all facets of the tech community, present and future. Underpinning everything is forging links with the wider community and this is a symbiotic relationship. Connecting with society brings three main advantages:

firstly spreading the word about training and working in technology. Secondly, connecting with like-minded people; and thirdly, giving back to local society.

So, with that, we created {CX}^{2} Talent Solutions.

{CX}^{2} = {Client Experience}{Candidate Experience}

The principle of customer experience centric cultures was key to the naming and ethos of our business. For us it encapsulated six key areas:

1. Understanding and Empathy

2. Engagement

3. Creativity

4. Values

5. Goal Setting

6. Community and Society

1. Understanding And Empathy

Within a traditional recruitment model, the only customer was the client not the candidate because the focus was always on the money not the best possible outcome, which meant that a candidate was treated like a commodity and merely spammed to any business. Nobody discussed whether the candidate was a good team fit and combined with the lack of consultation with either party the outcome was often poor in the long run.

We wanted to take all of our customers, both client and candidate on a customer journey. For us, it was obvious, you need to understand your customer's wants, but also their needs.

We purposefully named our business *Talent Solutions* not {CX}^{2} Recruitment Solutions, because we offer more than just recruitment, we offer a full-service.

We want our clients to feel as if we are part of their business, by understanding every facet of it and being able to take that knowledge to every candidate we speak to. Rather than just working from a job description and working with key technical terms and responsibilities we have a deep understanding of their needs and business culture. We listen to the client and the candidate to place the best candidate with the best business.

2. Engagement

It's traditional for a recruiter to want to engage with a client and a candidate, but how can you get the client and the candidate to engage with you, the recruiter?

If you can be genuine and honest, people will relate to you. Engagement doesn't just start at the beginning of the relationship/project, but throughout the experience. Engagement is not just about buy in, but communication. For example, if we haven't sent a CV yet, we keep the client updated with what we have done or what the market is doing. We ensure we are keeping them updated and in constant communication. Customers that trust you, will always remain engaged and this extends to the candidates. There does not always have to be a reason to give someone a call or email, they will always appreciate that contact, as a way of saying, we've not forgotten you.

3. Creativity

The traditional unique selling points in the recruitment industry are:

- We can deliver three CVS within 24-48 hours.
- We use all of the latest job boards.
- We have got an extensive database.

Our creativity was something we wanted to demonstrate to our customers, from social media marketing to topical podcasts, to tackling problems like the digital skills gaps and employee engagement, and for many recruitment businesses, unless the return was immediate, then it wasn't supported or valued.

As a tech based business, we had to be adopters of technology. Our client's and candidates are at the top of their game, they are technology leaders, so we had to set an example. From video technology to save candidates and client's time, to using Slack to help collaboration and communications internally. We've even managed to communicate with our candidates through WhatsApp when promoting client's and their marketing material.

The modern recruiter has to be a digital and social marketeer and we wanted to use tools that helped us to be more productive whilst putting out social content that was valuable to our audiences and that would keep them engaged with the work we were doing in the tech eco-system and community.

Creativity is key for helping us to stand out of that crowd. The creative use of technology has helped us discuss and transmit topics that highlight our personality and brand.

4. Values

Our values were completely fundamental to starting this journey, they include concepts such collaboration, clarity, and confidence.

We wanted to absorb any client's values that we chose to partner with, by looking for synergy between their values and ours, but more importantly in the modern employability world, candidates are no longer hired for just their ability to do a job, but also to embrace the company's cultures and values.

Equally important is the interview process, it is no longer focused on the client quizzing a candidate. This is a two-way relationship now, where it's as important for a client to sell and market themselves, especially in such a competitive industry as tech.

We said that our candidates are our customers too, and as a business we wanted to commit to them. We want to give them a true customer experience, rather than feeling like they are merely the middleperson in this whole "transaction".

We understand that moving jobs is one of the top four things you do in your life. It is our role to understand their wants and needs, sometimes acting as a life coach to discover what those are.

No client is the same, no candidate is the same. You should treat them with respect, and understand what their aspirations are, and guide them with integrity. If you help candidates in line with their expectations and reasons for wanting a new job, you are not only managing their job search well but helping them make one of life's biggest decisions.

5. Goal Setting

There is a phrase If you can't beat them join them. That was never our mindset. We didn't want to beat them or join them. We wanted to separate ourselves from other recruiters.

We set clear goals from the start, all of which had deadlines. Starting a business, it is easy to not focus on goals but it is vital.

> *"Dreams without goals are just dreams,*
> *and they ultimately fuel disappointment"*
> Denzel Washington

On the recruitment side, we set the standard goals: financials, new clients, number of meetings. But we set other goals; number of blogs, podcasts, weekly social content posting, video introductions and of course *How We Were Going To Bridge The Digital Skills Gap.*

Now we have attained these goals, so it's not what we were "going to do", we are able to talk about the actions we have taken and what we have achieved. We are able to talk about goals that have given back to society and our community when speaking to candidates and clients which gives us some credibility.

6. Community and Society

How do you stand out in a crowded market? We wanted to do something that hadn't been done before, and also something that would give us enjoyment.

We wanted to create something that was focused on the community and giving back, which is a polar opposite to an industry tarnished with being transactional and selfish. So we focused on bridging the digital skills gap and inspiring the next generation of future tech talent.

To illustrate our approach we created an eco-system of what we believe the words "community and society embodies".

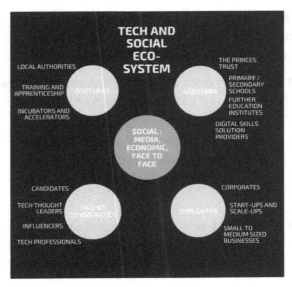

Originally we had an idea of what it was to be "community-focused" and many other businesses didn't understand this "new concept" but we have demonstrated this through our three Community Brands.

For us, it's about how much impact we have had on the community as a whole, and as we set up the business to improve our work/life balance, and not to be millionaires, but to leave a legacy.

Summary

You can shape and alter any industry despite what people tell you, if you stick to your vision and goals, it is possible to create real change. More importantly it is our duty to support the young people of today and future generations within any social milieu.

Everyone in society and the tech eco-system has a role to play in ensuring a future for young people and they are all responsible in ensuring that we have a healthy talent pipeline and that the talent has the ambitions and aspirations to be part of that pipeline. By focusing on the digital skills gap we are giving that support.

Using CX in our company name means we have to embody and commit to our values. We wanted to demonstrate our company values, through the commitment we give our clients and candidates and this is demonstrated through our actions and passion. If you really believe in an idea and a cause, it is your mission to take that idea and run with it, sometimes you will have to make a u-turn or hit a bump, but if you persevere you will achieve your goal.

Winning new customers for us, is now a by product because our focus has become the work we do in giving back to the community and the tech eco-system.

About Daniel Hoff-Rodrigues

Daniel Hoff-Rodrigues is the Founder of {CX}² Talent Solutions, a technology recruitment business supporting the community in Birmingham and the West Midlands. With ten years of industry experience, he set up the city's first community focused recruitment business that supports young people from all walks of life helping them to set goals and enter the tech sector. In 2018 he created The Brum Muse, a forum dedicated to bridging the digital skills gap in the city, and is the Community Lead for Digital Skills for Birmingham Tech Week.

Daniel and his business aim to support the community by keeping the talent and tech sector booming, but has big plans to support Diversity and Inclusion within digital and tech, giving more opportunities for BAME people and working with schools to focus on the way they inspire their pupils to seek a career in the tech and digital sector in the future.

To connect with Daniel

https://twitter.com/dan_techrecruit

https://www.linkedin.com/in/danrodrigues7

https://www.instagram.com/cx2talent

www.cx-squared.com

Customer Experience 2

The Three Key Dilemmas
Of Customer Experience

Gayana Helder

Let me take you back to a hot sunny day earlier this year. It was Day 2 of our Customer Experience Masterclass in Holland. I was presenting the last topic: *Culture*. A topic close to my heart.

The delegates and I were engaged, energised and passionate. A delegate raises his hand and asked, "Gayana, I think that all of us here - customer experience believers - are in agreement, however, how can I ensure that senior leadership truly believes in a Customer Centric Culture? They say they do, but when it gets tough .... ".

Immediately, another delegate echoes the same concern: "I recognise that I find myself justifying the return on investment of becoming a customer and employee centric organisation to our senior leadership over and over again".

A third participant adds: "My challenge is that we are operating in silos and have conflicting KPIs and objectives. How do I bring our Customer Experience team, sales, and the back office on one page, truly embedding Customer Centric way of working and culture?"

A knowing smile appears on my face. I was expecting these questions because it comes up regularly. These are the three most frequently raised questions during our Masterclasses.

There is no easy answer or a short cut but it all comes down to where you are, culturally, today; and the readiness of your organisation and leadership to embrace Customer Experience as an operational practice. Here's how I approach it.

Dilemma 1. Senior Leadership Says They Are True Believers But When It Gets Tough …

I remember feeling very frustrated with my senior leadership team in a previous role and shared this frustration with my husband. "Sounds like they are not on the same journey as you are."

I decided to try a different approach. I created a bottom-up program called *The Power of Enthusiasm* based on the book *The Super Promoter* and the *Super Promoter Methodology* by Rijn Vogelaar. The book is about the power of *enthusiasm*.

Superpromoters are enthusiastic about a brand, product or organisation; and their enthusiasm is contagious. Enthusiasm is vitally important because it links to customer engagement, increasing new clients and growth in turnover.

Superpromoters motivate the team and, ultimately, drive the positive reputation and sustained success of companies.

So I wrote an article in the monthly company magazine, looking for ambassadors - superpromoters - like me. To my surprise, I got 30 brave first-followers … and ambassadors.

Together we collected powerful stories from within our organisation: stories of employees that went above and beyond for our customers. And each month we shared these stories. Our Board of Directors were so impressed that soon they were actively asking for more of these enthusiastic stories; and started to participate in the program themselves.

This had an incredibly positive result of increasing both employee and senior leadership engagement.

To ensure that we collected real life customer and employee stories, we would literally bring the customer into our organisation during a quarterly business update. At the business update our CEO would facilitate a dialog based on the results.

I had surveyed all our employees asking them: *What is most valued, and most important for our customers?* They said:

- Expertise
- Relationship
- Trust.

What my colleagues didn't know is that I had asked the same questions to our customers. And do you know how our customers answered the same survey question?

- Trust
- Relationship
- Expertise.

That's what customers were enthusiastic about! So while our team saw the value of enthusiasm; they now patently saw the important need to include the needs and priorities of customers and what they were enthusiastic for.

The insights of this exercise were profound. Both parties were enthusiastic but not in the same order of importance. But the implications for our business became clear and elevated the decision to get behind the programs especially when things were tough!

Lesson Learned: To make a change, you sometimes have to be brave and show the potential of what can be achieved, and drive it, to make people believe.

Dilemma 2: Justifying The Return On Investment (ROI)

The power of listening to customers is well documented. Companies understand the need to collate what customers think about products and services and how they flag key improvements. And it is not too difficult to listen to a customer and gather real time feedback. We also know that text analytics can transform chaotic customer voice data into structured recommendations.

But acting on that data is hard. It costs time, money, resources, and needs effort. And deciding to spend money on making a business customer centric is not easy if the financial benefits are not easily understood. Does it drive revenues and profits and market share, for example?

The challenge is determining the most relevant metrics and in theory calculating the ROI should be relatively straightforward making it easy to validate the needs for creating experiences that are both customer and employee centric. But implementing insights is not as simple.

Let me give you an example how I got this wrong the first time.

In one of my first roles as Customer Experience Manager, I had made the business case to invest in an NPS measurement system, to help us collect and act on customer feedback. The initial results showed that there was a lot of room for improvement. After connecting this data to customer retention, I presented a compelling case that if we improve customer experience it would deliver us x% of business growth; and less churn. As you can imagine - I had the attention of senior leadership and they expected a solid ROI.

Having the data to support my proposal, I looked for a short delivery plan, quick impact, speed and build urgency. And I made the NPS scorecard a companywide initiative as one of the bonus components. There is a saying The Netherlands: *The bigger the steps, the sooner I am home.* Looking back, here's where I made my biggest mistake. I wanted to see financial benefits, sooner.

I quickly learned that although improving Customer Experience always leads to financial rewards, the best way is to *first* create an environment that can change. Your team must be able to *first* deliver the future model, *before* tying that to performance metrics or a bonus. If they fail, then this will only frustrate them and the whole organization, creating the wrong culture. A year later, I was still doing damage control, all because I tried to go too fast, too soon.

Lesson Learned: You can't take short cuts, even if the data tells you to. Having customer insights is not enough. You have to create an environment that understands the change *before* they can change. You are what you *do*, not what you *say* you do.

Dilemma 3: Operating In Silos With Conflicting Objectives And KPIs That Don't Align

This challenge is true for so many different scenarios, not just for CX. You need to take a step back and revisit the question: *What is your desired customer experience that you want to deliver?* Once you know exactly what you want your customers *to feel* *then* you translate it to your Customer Journey.

Two key insights are 1) focus on structuring the organization based on the Customer Journey with a focus on aligning the various silos; and 2) help all employees to understand the role they play in delivering the desired Customer Experience across the company. The real game-changer is to help your employees experience and understand the parts of the other contributors.

I learned to appreciate the classical dilemma between the head and the heart. It's not enough to create an awareness of their own role. That's why I initiated a program called *Pay a visit to...* As an example, have a sales representative exchange roles with a customer service representative. This allows them to experience the promises we make to our customers, across the different departments during the different conversations we have with our customers. This allows them to see things from different perspectives and to better appreciate why we need to work together; and to see ourselves one company not silos.

This is very true from an IT perspective as well, where passing of transactions and data between departments can create data silos. So when a customer calls for some information, departments often say *Sorry that's not my area* and pass them around the company. Having an efficient IT solution to support your employees, who support your customers is key. This is a very important way to break down the silo's and together bring the desired Customer Experience form paper to life.

Lesson Learned: H.E. Luccock said, "No one can whistle a symphony alone. It takes a whole orchestra to play it". We can align KPIs, but the real magic happens when your employees understand their own and the other's part to be played.

Summary

So coming back to my story, and where I started. CX practitioners are often concerned about how they will overcome these three *do we or don't we* dilemmas. In my experience, these can be overcome by adopting the solutions I have shared with you in the examples.

- Create a movement bottom up and inspire senior leadership team to actively participate.

- Choose to not be blind for the power of enthusiasm as a company.

- Share real-life customer stories.

- You are what you do, not what you say. Making courageous and uncomfortable decisions is part of the deal.

- Align with the Customer Journey and ensure every employee understands the role they and all other contributors play in delivering the desired customer experience.

About Gayana Helder

Gayana Helder is a certified customer experience professional (CCXP), public speaker and the managing director of NeCXus, a customer experience management consultancy and training firm, providing Customer Experience Masterclasses, in-house and as a public course.

Gayana is a spirited customer experience leader, who is passionate about humanizing businesses, transforming companies to a customer centric one, bringing the desired customer experience to life and encourages human centric leadership.

Previously, Gayana worked for Dell, fulfilling several business improvement and change management roles within Dell EMEA for six years. Gayana has helped the Dutch Yellow Pages to transform to a customer centric online marketing provider.

Currently, Gayana is the Global Vice President Inside Sales, also heading Global Customer Service & Customer Experience Strategy for IWG Group.

www.necxus.agency

https://www.linkedin.com/in/gayanahelder

Customer Centric Culture: The Only Strategic Competitive Advantage. How To Measure And Manage It

Olga Guseva

Corporate culture is the only feature that can't be copied by the competition, and it is the only long-lasting advantage that will stay with you despite all market changes and disruptions. This may sound like a bold statement until you take a moment and think how many unique products and services you can currently name in your market. In case a truly innovative product appears, the competition is catching up quickly and in no time you have a range of alternatives. Think iPhone, Xerox or Pampers. Those brands have been so unique, that the name of the brand became the name of the product – and look, they are far from being unique now. Customer-centric corporate culture is your only strategic and lasting competitive advantage that can differentiate you.

Why Worry About Customer Centric Culture?

Stop and consider for a moment: If the culture of your workplace was to become as good as it realistically could, how much improvement would there be on people's performance/ productivity? If you are like many business leaders across the world, in accordance with Steve Simpson's research (Simpson S., Du Plessis S. (2018). A Culture Turned: Using UGRs to boost performance and culture. Keystone Management Services), you would land with an average number somewhere around 40%.

Just think about it – business leaders across the world believe that corporate culture has a potential to almost double the commercial performance. Would that mean it is worth exploring and developing?

Surprisingly, close results have been received during a comprehensive academic study conducted by the team led by Dr. Linden Brown from MarketCulture (Brown L., Brown C. (2013). *The Customer Culture Imperative: A Leader's Guide to Driving Superior Performance*. McGraw-Hill Education). The researchers discovered a strong positive correlation between strong customer-centric corporate culture and more than 35 key business performance indicators, including ROI, profit, sales volume, ability to innovate and expand to new markets. More than 50% of commercial success of the company is explained by the strength of the customer-centric corporate culture.

Easy To Say, Hard To Do

The link seems natural and obvious. So, if a customer-centric culture is that important, why do so many companies struggle to build it? In my view, because corporate culture cannot be touched, seen or heard. Executives are typically well prepared to manage "tangible things" like business processes and products, but they can get stuck when confronted by the "fluffy cloud" that does not have shape, beginning, end or any physical attributes. What gets measured gets managed, but how do you make customer centric culture measurable?

A Way To Measure

The team of Dr. Linden Brown have been looking for the answer and over 10 years of research has resulted in a practical tool called the Market Responsiveness Index (MRI™). The MRI™ has been used by more than 400 companies worldwide (*https:// www.marketculture.com/mri*).

The idea behind it is very simple: behaviour reflects the culture. By understanding the behaviour and then building the right "habits" within the company, theoretically, we can make corporate culture more customer centric.

The research has defined eight disciplines that fully and sufficiently describe all major characteristics of a customer centric culture. By analysing these disciplines and working on them as they relate to your company, you can better identify the priorities and build a sound development plan for the weaker areas and support for the stronger ones.

For convenience, all eight disciplines are represented in a circular diagram. The better each specific discipline is developed within the company, the bigger the coloured part of the corresponding sector becomes.

Let's have a look at Figure 1 and take a tour around the customer centric corporate culture.

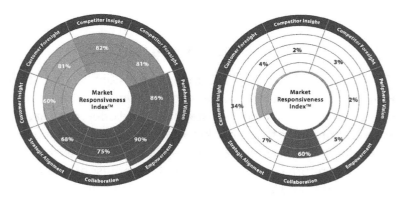

Figure. 1. MRI™ (Market Responsiveness Index): examples of companies with high and low level of customer centricity.

It's All About Customer

The first two disciplines - Customer Insight, Customer Foresight - are related to customers. The ability of the company to understand current customer needs, wishes and aspirations may seem obvious, but what is equally important is whether the company is acting in accordance with this understanding. Do the research data and customer journey maps become a wall decoration, or is the company acting upon them?

The ability to understand and anticipate future customer needs now or sooner, allows you to develop products and services that will win customers' hearts in three, five, or even ten years time.

It allows you to consider: Will my customers be the same but just growing older, getting married and having kids? What will they need? What will be important to them? Will their needs change? Or, will it be a new generation with different lifestyle and consumption trends? Customer foresight gives you clarity as to what consumers will need in the future and what you should be doing right now to be better prepared to meet those anticipated needs.

Competitors Are Crucial

The next two disciplines - Competition Insight, Competition Foresight - are related to competition. Understanding your current competition helps you stay afloat and offer relevant and attractive products to the market. As always, it is not enough to understand, it is important to action – change pricing, packaging, delivery or return conditions, waiting time or response rates to stay attractive and profitable today. Competitor foresight is all about future competitors. They can be your old acquaintances that you know for ages or the products and companies that come from completely different markets. The biggest threat to airlines, selling transatlantic flights, came not from the airline industry, but from increasing popularity of video conferencing.

The market of still-shot cameras have been killed by smartphones, and the photo-printing industry has been replaced by social media. Competitor foresight gives you time to act and get prepared for the future competitive landscape.

What's In The Periscope?

Peripheral vision is the ability of the company to see and understand the political, economic, social, legal, technological, environmental and all other aspects of external environment that influence the company. Not only understand, but undertake practical steps in accordance with this understanding. The COVID-19 pandemic is probably the best example of such an influence. The companies who managed to recognise the early signs of the situation and acted upon it - built remote workplaces, moved fast to digital environment, helped consumers to adapt, came up with new product and service offerings relevant to the situation – those are the ones who will make it into the future.

Looking Inside

The last-but-not-least section contains three disciplines - Empowerment, Collaboration, Strategic Alignment - that relate to internal processes and behaviours within the organisation. Employee empowerment is a pre-requisite of good customer service. Ability to understand what can be done for the customer here and now and willingness to actually do it without lengthy communication with management, defines the ability of the company to create great consumer experiences in ever changing conditions.

Collaboration between different departments is also vital. Most customer experience tasks can't be resolved by one department and require cross-functional collaboration. It could be IT + Finance, Accounting + Sales or Customer Support + Manufacturing. The combinations are endless, but all require good understanding of customer needs and true readiness and willingness to cooperate.

Strategic alignment crowns the list of eight crucial disciplines that define customer centric culture. Ability of the employees to understand company strategy, mission and values and relate them to their daily tasks define whether the strategy will actually be executed or not.

The "How To": An Action Guide

MRI™ can be used for measuring the strengths of the customer centric culture of the company, giving the so-wanted numerical values that can help tracking progress or benchmarking against others. It serves as a strategic guidance, highlighting the areas where the culture is already rather strong (for example, the Empowerment discipline on the left diagram on Picture 1 above). It also helps find the zones where company needs to improve (the Customer Insight discipline on the left diagram for example).

To measure the level of customer centricity, the data is collected online from company employees. This means that upon the completion of the survey the company is in possession of a whole bank of ideas collected directly from its own staff that knows from deep inside what is working and what could have been done better. Analysis of sub-cultures of different divisions or layers of management can also bring important insights and revelations.

We use this tool a lot to help companies understand where they are now and what are the next most vital steps. A large logistics company discovered their growth zone in the empowerment discipline. As a result, they have initiated a change program giving more authority to the regional directions. A company working in the IT services industry has discovered that while the employees are acting in accordance with the strategy, there's a lack of involvement and clarity as to how strategic goals shall be translated into daily tasks – they are now taking actions to bring the implementation of their strategy to full strength.

MRI™ is not just a measurement tool. It is a philosophy with a proven correlation to commercial success. Every company can use the MRI philosophy to access different aspects of its corporate culture and improve them. Try using it as a framework for your next strategic meeting. Ask yourself and your colleagues, which behaviours you see across each discipline, what is working great and what could be done better. Share the best practices across your company and create an action plan to fill in the gaps. Make your customer centric culture grow stronger day by day and watch your customer experience is improving. Start writing your own success story today!

About Olga Guseva

Olga Guseva is a CX strategy consultant, certified MRI™ customer culture management and transformation specialist.

She is one of the few CXPA recognised training providers globally, first CCXP in Russia, MBA, PhD., keynote speaker and blogger.

Olga is a judge and ambassador of several international CX competitions, including International CX Awards, CX World Awards, CX Leader of the Year, European CX Awards and DACH CX Awards.

She is the co-author of the *Customer Experience* book, Amazon bestseller in several countries in Customer Service category in 2019.

Olga is based in Russia and manages Integria Consult, a consulting company providing training, measurement and consulting services.

www.integriaconsult.ru

olga@integriaconsult.ru

https://www.linkedin.com/in/olgaguseva

More information on award winning MRI™ philosophy and measurement tool can be found at MarketCulture Inc:

https://www.marketculture.com/mri

2. Organisation Adoption And Accountability

Having clear priorities and accountability in an continuous improvement environment

Customer Experience 2

The Future Is Now

Ruth Crowley

Courage is what it takes to stand up and speak.
Courage is also what it takes to sit down and listen.
Winston Churchill

Companies have historically considered a one to three year plan. It always sounds good: - forward looking and strategic to stakeholders. However, history shows three year objectives either moved out or were never completed. Current industry trends, economic headwinds and a challenging business environment dictate the need for change now. The COVID 19 pandemic changed the trajectory compounding challenges in every business sector. What began as a health crisis created a business crisis. The human and economic impact was devastating. A significant outcome for business was the need for urgency and immediate acceleration of plans.

We can no longer wait for the right time – now is the right time. The current environment calls for urgent patience. The future plan must include Customer Experience, considering the Customer as a valued asset and experience improvement as part of the growth strategy. It requires Design Thinking starting with empathy to develop what matters most for the Customer. Design Planning will get to the best answer, beyond a linear value chain considering the entire ecosystem, not to mimic current process or validate executive beliefs, but expanding the aperture for a broader, clearer view. Design Planning helps integrate the trifecta of business factors, technical capability and user value: the future plan.

Design Planning and Customer Experience Design are rooted in facts, employing a holistic view with a disciplined process to understand all options available to the Customer. Defining minimum, viable and desirable solutions to differentiate and augment the business offer. The rigor in the process helps frame the problem beyond symptoms, describing the problem before prescribing the solution, or rushing to an answer. It is less about margin and more about value creation and anticipating changing Customer needs. It's not a project, it's a mission. Fundamentally, we are in the people business. The Customer has to be at the centre.

Facts Supporting Change

The World Economic Forum in 2016 estimated the value of current digital transformation to business and society will top $100 Trillion by 2025. Businesses are behind. We call it Digital Darwinism. Technology is moving faster than businesses can keep up. Leveraging data and applying technology to align with the business model (and capital plan) helps mobilize change.

In 2005 Bain and Co. found that 80% of CEO's believed they were delivering a superior experience. When they asked Customers of those companies about their perceptions, only

8% agreed. In 2018 and 2019 Forrester and Lumoa repeated the study. Results were only minimally better with 18% agreement. The gap represents opportunity which is real but not realized.

85% of Customers will pay up to 25% more to ensure a superior experience. Conversely, over 70% will tell others about a bad experience. With social media, bad news travels fast. 48% of shoppers left a website and purchased from a competitor because of a poor personalized experience. Retail Touchpoints benchmark studies reported 55% demand more customized 1:1 experiences. 92% of consumers worldwide trust recommendations from friends and family more than any form of advertising (up from 74% in 2007). The London School of Economics found there is a 300% revenue gain by reducing negative word-of-mouth vs. increasing positive "buzz". GDPR and privacy regulations require mindfulness. However, 64% of Customers approve of companies storing purchase history and data, if it results in additional personalized experiences (BRP Consultants). 74% of Customers are more likely to purchase on line if they can return or exchange in store. Customers who shop across channels have a higher lifetime value (up to 30%). There are countless studies validating the value and impact of Customer Experience. Results are the outcome of creating and delivering optimal experiences.

Customers encounter more impressions than they can process or remember. There is more data available on mobile devices than NASA teams had for the first mission to the moon (Madrigal 2019). The delivery system is more complicated and pressured, including last mile delivery in retail. With the proliferation of options the Customer is intolerant of interactions not aligned with their specific needs. More than ever, they have the power to reject what doesn't work for them.

Vision and well-captured mission statements are worthless without action. Change requires leadership alignment and commitment, with purposeful integration and synchronization at all touchpoints across the ecosystem. It is not a tweak.

It requires correction. A unified review of touchpoints across the Customer journey increases ability to understand behaviour patterns, drive relevant engagement and upsell opportunities, anticipate gaps and correct pain points. The Customer experience across channels should be seamless and frictionless vs. a series of disparate, disconnected, fragmented elements. A consistent, cohesive, unified experience helps forge enduring relationships, connecting with Customers where they are, now and in the future.

The essence of experience architecture is working effectively in the moment while creating the framework for the future. It happens on a continuum which requires relentless focus. It's not a project but a process, not instant but constant, necessitating a change in mindset. As previously stated, Customer Experience, especially now, is not an initiative but an imperative.

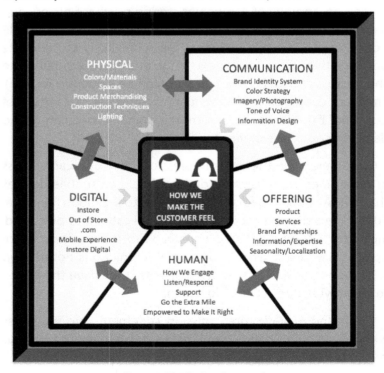

Figure 1: The Project Approach

Cross Functional Integration

Every time you are tempted to react in the same old way, ask if you want to be a prisoner of the past of a pioneer of the future.
Deepak Chopra

Breaking functional silos is challenging and generally meets with resistance. The value of leveraging cross-disciplinary expertise is fundamental for success. Leaders must set the example cultivating a purpose-driven, learning mindset. It's not about dictation as much as orchestration and mobilization. Simplifying the process to amplify the experience, intentionally shaping interactions with the Customer, moving from quick fixes to viable, feasible, desirable (then scalable) solutions. Moving from fragmented formats to unified systems and a functional perspective to an enterprise view, promotes optimal digital, physical and human experiences. Democratizing data so associates have access to the same information as the Customer, enables connection. Consider human factors. Emotion drives behaviour. If Customers and Associates are emotionally involved and engaged, results are the outcome. Collaboration is multiplication.

In a prior role, the CXD Group did extensive work to elevate the Customer Experience in two core categories. We did all the right work including Customer and associate research, observation and journey mapping from the on-line research phase to the after sale. We leveraged data, analytics and insights, studied best-in-class emulators. We illustrated the total experience journey to identify gaps (opportunities). We employed Human Centred Design methodology to observe, interpret, frame and solve. We synthesised journey maps which showed the pain points experienced by the Customer and the associates were inextricably linked. Addressing and correcting the end-to-end delivery ecosystem could result in doubling the business. Then we hit the "functional barriers" which almost stopped the work.

It's why I advocate we cannot allow the vertical lines of the organisation structure get in the way of the horizontal Customer process.

Long story short, the digital group questioned "what makes you think you know better" and "who gets credit if it works"? We had to negotiate. (Internal negotiation is a big vacuum in CX). We collaborated and co-created. We learned together which made it better. We put the Customer at the centre. The trepidation felt was real and a function of organisational culture. People were afraid of being undermined. Collaboration generated an 1100% increase in hits in week one and triple digit increases beyond that. The Team was energised – and got full credit! A postscript: results went down after the second month as the Team was redirected to the next "emergency". A failure in leadership commitment, staying the course to serve the Customer. In all initiatives, continuation is as important as activation. Relationships require continuity to fortify the foundation. The process has to provide an emotional navigation system enabling all parts of the organisation to do what they do best, delivering unified and consistent experiences at all touchpoints, not just occasionally, but continuously.

Experiential listening provides radical clarity and an unfiltered data source. Incorporating the "Go to the Gimba" (go and see) practice provides a lens on what it's like to walk in the Customer's shoes. Valuing the perspective of the Customer and the people serving the Customer, including  them in solution co-creation, builds momentum and trust to fuel growth. It is an iterative process where small wins are celebrated and measured and the journey continues.

One of the biggest mistakes we make as leaders is to assume we know the answer, we know what has to be done. The pace of change in the industry would say it is impossible to be all-knowing. While our experience serves as a good base of reference, we have to be open to change. Life (and business) is a learning laboratory. Are we consciously creating, adapting and evolving or sleepwalking and reacting to change? The future requires organisational change.

Change requires humility, tenacity, courage, fortitude and the willingness to believe the answers are only found after asking the right questions, moving from tactical execution ("how do we") to strategic ideation ("how might we"). The future calls for urgent patience to create unified, seamless and contactless touchpoints where the Customer can engage on their terms. Contactless does not mean "hands off". Experience is high touch, heart and soul. Finding the right equilibrium (solving the right problem) is where the magic happens.

As a pioneer of the future, it would be a tragedy to invest your heart and soul in a compromise.

About Ruth Crowley

Ruth Crowley has been a Customer Experience advocate with iconic brands including Lowe's Home Improvement (Fortune 100), Harley-Davidson, Universal Studios, M&M Mars, Nickelodeon and Host Marriott, in the U.S. and Global markets. She has worked across industries including Retail, Travel and Hospitality, Entertainment, Theme Parks, Brand Design and Licensing.

Currently Ruth works with the Hudson Group a division of Dufry International, the largest travel retailer in the world. She has experience across functions including Customer Experience Design, Store Design, Product and Concept Design, Merchandising, Licensing, Business Development, Operations and Brand Strategy.

Yet, Ruth says she is a continuing student in a universe evolving at warp speed. She articulates the need for continuous learning and expanding skillsets to create relevant solutions that elevate human experience, differentiate Brands and optimise results.

Ruth is proud of her Board service applying diverse experience supporting people and business. She is actively involved with the University of North Texas College of Merchandising, Hospitality and Travel. She serves on the Advisory Board, as Student mentor and Executive in Residence.

Mobile: (US) +1 407- 488-6080

freespirit259@aol.com

linkedin.com/in/ruth-crowley-1598718

CX Transformation -
From Design To Implementation & Adoption

Spiros Milonas

OK, so you have reached a point where you realise that you want (or need) to build a customer centric organisation. You have attended presentations and read articles, case studies and books (including the one you are holding) for guidance and inspiration. You have identified metrics, tools -such as journey mapping- and have even designed a CX program.

Organisation adoption and accountability usually refers to "who does what" so that there is enough clarity, accountability and ownership. Here is the deal: in this chapter we will go beyond this important process and instead highlight the elements that people leading Customer Experience transformation should keep in mind in order to go from talking, planning and trying to transform to actually transforming.

No transformation is easy as it refers to a profound change. Using the definition of Deborah Rowland from her book *Still Moving*, "change is the disturbance of repeating patterns", so by definition it is a disturbing process since it usually involves resistance due to known or unknown loyalties. If it were that easy we would all effortlessly make the shift from "how we stand now" to "how we want to stand". And for that shift (change) to happen we need -to put it boldlyto **betray** and **abandon** all those patterns that have brought us to where we are today.

Change happens outside of our comfort zone so this is exactly why individuals and organisations want to settle to what is familiar. The objective of this chapter is not to discourage you, but rather give you a heads up for what is ahead, should you decide to transform your business, along with ways that can make this journey as smooth as possible.

Organisations are living vibrant entities. We use the word organisations -from the word organisms- because ever since they were created (or born if you may) they breathe, grow and evolve. Their culture is developed while growing, similar to how your own personality is cultivated. In other words, organisations are not legal soulless entities with a tax ID number, but rather living vibrant systems that start forming their substance from the day they are conceived.

Acknowledging The Need For Change

The first step for making a shift is "Acknowledging the need for change". On a personal level there is something that triggers your need for change. In a business the need might be identified only by some members of the system yet the chances for a successful transformation are greater if the founders (parents), leadership (guardians) and the majority of the employees (family) are behind it. This is crucial as the intention (clarity, acceptance, motivation) is what will fuel the organisation's shift. Now when it comes to customer experience, make sure you have a "critical mass" acknowledging and desiring that need for change. Use data and case studies from other companies or even competitors, that will make them understand and agree on the business need. Observe what the organisation you serve truly values and try to link that with the change you are advocating. If it values profits talk about ROI and CX, if it values public image and PR talk about the effect CX can have in creating and sharing stories, and if it values hierarchy talk about how the leadership can focus less on micromanagement by adjusting the role of the team. Just look closely at what the organisation truly values rather than what it says it values. No judgment. Only then you can make your case for CX so that there will be enough "charge" for people to deal with that uncomfortable change which will follow.

Acknowledging What Is

The second step is "Acknowledging what is". Diagnosing and identifying the whole picture (including blind spots) is of great value in order to find out what you are TRULY dealing with. When it comes to Customer Experience, you can use a combination of things: internal questionnaires to the whole team, ask one or more questions to customers to identify a potential perception gap, interviews, etc. It is important that you find ways to map the "as is" based on different perspectives. When it comes to blind spots the systemic lens can be of great service. Let me share a bit more on that:

We are a result of what we are surrounded by. We belong in systems that have their ordering forces, the rules based on which they operate. Every organisation is a living system. The four main ordering forces of human systems as articulated by Bert Hellinger, are related to:

- events that have happened in the **course of time** and have left their mark,

- the extent to which everyone has the right **place** in the system,

- the balance in all that is **exchanged** and registered by the system's intuitive sense of what is owed or deserved as well as

- including everything that needs to **belong** so that the system feels complete

Usually entanglements in systems, including organisations, lie and relate to one of those ordering forces. I will share two examples. The first of a telecoms company which had people fired (including the management) for being involved in a financial scandal. Although we might feel something does not have a place in our organisation (rebels, jokers, events that have caused pain or embarrassment in the course of time like in this case) systems have the tendency to include all that is excluded to be complete. So, in this case, gradually initiatives and accountability declined as people connected to that chapter being entangled in an unconscious state that said "we are too embarrassed to put ourselves out there...we do not deserve to thrive having caused (financial) damage and acted unethically".

A second example was a company that created a position around CX to satisfy a handful of people who felt strongly about it and were quite vocal. The result was that the need for a CX function was not really acknowledged by the organisation. A person is in service of a function and not the other way round (a function in service of the person). As a result the person held a position that did not have a place in the organisation and CX started to become idle.

Knowing your organisations' patterns as part of the "as is" is very important when trying to design a CX transformation. Identifying blind spots following this theory would require much more than a chapter. For now, please keep in mind that gathering different perspectives as well as looking beyond the surface are important in order to know your actual "as is". Before trying to change your "what is" make sure you stay with it, honour it and accept it rather than criticise it and reject it before you move on.

Planning For Change

The third step would be "planning for change". Designing the necessary actions (on measurement, VOC, design and improvement) and interventions (on culture, strategy). Two important elements to consider: firstly, when it comes to a profound change such as Customer Experience culture do not expect you can simply delegate change. Instead try **to co-create it with people that have acknowledged the need for change** and are connected with what you try to do. Tap into the collective intelligence of the group and ask people to join in contributing or at least being heard in designing the next day. Secondly, less is more in the sense that rather than designing many different initiatives that hopefully some will do the trick, **design fewer deeper more impactful interventions while providing the space for processing, reactions and inputs.** To use again Deborah Rowland's wording there is a clear difference between action and movement. Very often we get trapped in actions that usually keep us in our current state and serve our loyalties. It can be a combination of very impressive trainings, workshops, programs, you name, instead of carefully designed interventions followed by observation that will allow the system to shift.

Rolling Out

The fourth step would be **"Rolling out" and putting the plan into action.** This is also critical as you need to be alert and adapt the plan based on the system's reactions to what is happening. The collective intelligence of the organisation will naturally **want to settle at its comfort zone and what is known.** Adjusting the plan and having clarity on what is expressed in any way is crucial. The interventions will create a movement within the system and it is important to ensure that this movement is not blocked but rather nurtured at the pace that the system can manage. Hold lightly the plan and be ready to focus on what truly matters. In this phase everything that happens is valuable information. I have worked with organisations that put things on hold because other priorities or even crises came up. But it wasn't really about the crises or misprioritisation. At a deeper level the organisations were simply not ready for that shift yet. They needed space and time for processing and this had to be respected, otherwise any attempt for change would simply fall through. Building a customer led organisation cannot be enforced. So the plan is there to provide you and the team a sense of safety while stepping into unknown territory. You only need to insist on the end goal rather than the path. Observe, adjust and mindfully respond.

Embedding The Change

The last step would be **"Embedding the change"** into the system's DNA and creating a new reality. In this step it is important to offer the necessary support that will allow the internal "movement" to continue and really land rather than being blocked. At this stage, elements such as internal communication in order to share stories and foster new behaviours, linking KPIs and benefits with CX as well as the leadership acting as role models are absolutely crucial.

There is no right or wrong when it comes to transformations and each organisation (along with its members) decides for its future and fate. Life is about movement and this is exactly why adopting changes can be challenging yet needed.

About Spiros Milonas

Spiros Milonas is the founder of KRATAION Consulting, a boutique consulting agency based in Athens, Greece. Spiros studied Business Administration and holds an MBA from Instituto de Empresa in Spain where he graduated as part of the Dean's Class. He has broad commercial experience in various organisations in Europe. The last position in the corporate world before founding Krataion Consulting in 2011 was "Head of Sales for South East Europe" at Sony Ericsson. He started his own business in order to help organisations reach sustainable growth happiness and freedom. His approach synthesises different methodologies and tools to help businesses (from the biggest multinationals to startups) transform and manage their change and growth successfully.

He loves travelling and is a firm believer that business can be fun.

Website: www.krataionconsulting.com

Linkedin Profile: https://www.linkedin.com/in/spiros-milonas-96648b3

Email: spiros@krataionconsulting.com

Using Agility And Collaboration To Create Effective CX Believers

Olga Potaptseva

If you want to achieve big things like changing an organisation, you often need to create believers who will not only join you, but also help drive your vision. In this discussion I want to share with you how I use agility and collaborative strategies to achieve big changes.

Changing your organisational culture, getting investment for CX projects, or transforming operations is not directly comparable to the work of remarkable people like Malala Yousafzai, Nelson Mandela or Jane Austen but you too are changing the world. Like them, you may have started a revolution or worked quietly behind the scenes to create a CX conductive environment. Like them, you may feel lonely and powerless at times, but with the right motivation, tools and engagement you have a great chance to succeed in making the world a more customer centric place.

Bringing Disruption To People's Agenda Is Never Fun Or Popular – How Do You Get Your Key Stakeholders To Accept That You Have A Point?

Speaking their language is key to not being the odd one out. I used to work for a UK insurance company where, like in many similar companies, the Underwriters had for many years been responsible for the profit and loss at the company level. As you may imagine starting any focus on CX was not possible without the Underwriting Director's support, who in turn thought it unimaginable to focus on customer needs, satisfaction, and behaviours without a solid numerical reason. For four years, I turned up to any meeting he would have me, getting a good understanding of his agenda and prepared with customer insights. One glorious summer day, to my triumph, he could not explain a drop in the renewal rates with price fluctuations, whilst I could do it using the ethnographic research my team had done. We finally found a synergy and spoke the same language!

Finding synergies with your key business stakeholders is fundamental in terms of getting them to accept the CX strategy and actions, but it does not have to take you four years. Based on my experience, I recommend you keep abreast of the following:

- Key elements of your business strategy and meaningful business KPIs

- Individual KPIs of your potential sponsor or sponsors

- Objectives your CX strategy or project will help to achieve, such as value creation, cost reduction or revenue generation

- The business risks you are helping to avoid or are potentially creating

Build your CX-critical conversations as the best salesperson would, by asking situational questions first, proceeding to problem questions, then identification questions and finally steering questions. Lots of questions is the best tool for convincing, if asked in the right way!

If you are wondering what are the kind of questions that you should be asking, then let me share four different types of questions you may want to use.

1. Situational questions are designed to encourage an assessment of the current circumstances, such as ability to achieve targets, collaboration, focus, etc.

- Do we focus on delivering what our customers want and are ready to pay for?

- Do we have a robust understanding of what our customers would want next year or in three years?

- Do we understand why our customers stay with us? Do we use this in our retention strategy?

- Do we understand how well our competitors are meeting customer needs and why our customers may be switching/ buying from them?

- Are we clear why our customers own X products per customer and understand how to increase that?

2. Problem questions are there to ensure understanding of the problems that arise due to the current situation.

- What are the consequences of us not understanding our customers' needs?

- Are we confident our innovation budget will be used to its best potential if we do not know what our competitors are doing/ what our customers will want in future?

- What is the impact of us not having a clear view of why our customers stay with us or switch on our renewal rates?

- How confident are we that our improvement initiatives are targeting what matters to customers?

3. Identification questions – these questions allow you to understand how critical are the problems that we experience due to the lack of customer centricity or a particular CX project.

- What are the implications for your KPIs / ability to meet your targets?

- How does it influence our development as an organisation?

- How likely are we to see disruption in our industry in the next 3-5 years and would we be able to compete with new entrants?

- Are we being true to our mission?

- What is the impact on our employees?

4. Steering questions – these questions help you to identify the readiness of your potential sponsor to take specific action to facilitate the change.

- What would you personally be willing to do to support this initiative to avoid the negative implications you just mentioned/ achieve the positives?

- What would prevent us from launching this project?

- What are the barriers for execution in terms of engagement? How would you suggest we involve the management and the employees?

- When do you think we might be able to launch this project?

There Is Only One Of You And You Need CX Allies To Drive Your CX Agenda Forward - How Do You Get Them Onboard?

Congratulations, you have got the nod and some money for your projects. If, like the vast majority of CX teams, you have an aspiration to improve the end-to-end journey and a limited number of team members, you would have a hard time doing it all yourself. Plus, CX is all about collaboration, but how do you get your cross-functional teams engaged and working effectively? Management buy in is essential, but not enough. In my career I have built and led teams in CX, but my true team was the entire organisation and I could not do without everyone.

With a few bumps and bruises I discovered a set of five engagement principles to get all colleagues on board:

1. **CX as part of life, not an extra burden** - Fit around their agenda by demonstrating how CX could help them achieve their goals and use existing forums to avoid meeting fatigue

2. **You are on their side and listening, not disrupting** - Volunteer to support their projects that ultimately contribute to the end-to-end customer journey and deploy design thinking to find solutions to customer problems

3. **You contribute positively** - Choose your customer insights to provide the bits of the puzzle they are missing

4. **They still own 'their' CX** - Let them take the credit for improving the customer experience

5. **They deserve the praise** - Make them look good in the eyes of the management, colleagues, partners, and customers

Now people are excited, but will they keep going? Most likely not, unless you get them into a workflow rhythm

Great achievement, you have got the buy-in from the management and a strong desire from your colleagues to work collaboratively. Then 'business as usual' sets in and it all goes back to the good (bad) old time. To prevent this from happening and ensure continuous teamwork I use the principles of agile management in my CX practice.

- No micro-management. Provide the guidance, knowledge, and the tools for teams to be self-sufficient

- At all times maintain effective communication with all team members and stakeholders, including the customers

- Drive sustainable change by aligning CX projects scope, objectives and resources with the broader organisational agenda

- Simplicity is essential. Whenever trying to bring your point across use 'say it in 7' principle meaning that no slide can have more the seven bullet points, better still three or five

- Involve employees to find the key problems and the best solutions to them

These are great principles, but without the practical application mechanisms, they would be rather challenging to follow. So, where do you start? Would you be surprised if I told you that most companies are not sufficiently rigorous in defining the problems they're attempting to solve and articulating why those issues are important?

As a result, not only do they waste resources on doing something they shouldn't have needed to do, they also create organisational chaos and disengagement. As Albert Einstein once said: "If I were given one hour to save the planet, I would spend 59 minutes defining the problem and one minute resolving it".

To help you define the right problem before you engage your colleagues to resolve it, use these simple strategies:

1. Why does it need to be done? – think about how it fits into your CX strategy, business strategy, opportunities and risks of not doing

2. What do you expect as a result?

3. Write a project description starting with an action verb, e.g. prepare, do, agree, decide, organise, ensure. Verbs you shouldn't use: talk, call, discuss

4. Ensure your project description has at least 5 words – what needs to be achieved or done, where and for whom, what condition needs to be fulfilled

5. Make sure it is clear if read in two years' time

6. Adding expected result is a must – this will set the right expectations

7. Add a timeline

8. Write down the first action (ideally fill this in after the Engagement stage, together with your project sponsor)

Template

Project name	
Reason why	
Expected result	
Project description	Use action verb to start
	More than 5 words
	Add a timeline
	Add expected result
First step	

Once the problem has been defined and your cross-functional team have agreed the steps needed to resolve it, ensure keeping to a dynamic working rhythm, with clear daily objectives, accountability and SMART weekly objectives. Companies I work with tend to agree that daily 'stand up' 15-minute meetings help the project team to focus, minimise disruption, resolve any barriers quickly, re-focus if needed and generate tangible weekly progress. This in turn demonstrates progress and a sense of achievement to the team members who remain your CX believers who actually do the work.

Summary

Effective CX believers are your allies in delivering winning customer experiences. To keep them engaged you need to demonstrate how CX initiatives help them to achieve their objectives. Applying a business lens to what you do, effective engagement methods and agile working practices will create a 'team beyond the team' that organically ensures CX focus becomes a standard practice across the entire organisation.

Recommended Reading

- Are You Solving the Right Problem? by Dwayne Spradlin Harvard Business Review, September 2012

About Olga Potaptseva

Olga is a Founding Director for the European Customer Consultancy, supporting major brands across the globe in their customer-focussed business transformation. Having started her career with one of the Top5 market research companies she realised that far too often valuable insights get shelved without generating a much-needed change. With her faith in real customer centricity, she sought a highly challenging position of the Customer Experience Head with one of the UK insurers. For six years, she relentlessly focused on driving customer centricity and succeeded in turning the culture around to deliver business success through satisfying customer needs. Olga's in-depth expertise in setting up effective Voice of the Customer programs and driving sustainable insight-led change now helps her clients in the UK, Europe, Middle East, Far East and Russia. She is an Executive Director for the Customer Institute, a regular Chair of Judges at the UK and Middle East customer experience awards, a speaker and one of the Top25 CX Influencers of 2019.

Email: olga@eucustomerconsultancy.com

LinkedIn: www.linkedin.com/in/olga-potaptseva

Website: www.eucustomerconsultancy.com

From Customer Service To Customer Care – Organisational Alignment To Create Better Customer Outcomes.

Nick Lygo-Baker

By definition; if you have a customer, then you are providing a "customer experience". When people interact with you and your business then they will go through a customer journey and have customer outcomes. We live in a world of individuated consumption, where choice is infinite and customers expect a personalised experience. Brands, Retailers and Service Providers are constantly seeking the ideal formula to meet as many of these expectations with as little operational effort (and cost) as possible – right?!

But just wait a minute! Are we chasing an impossible dream? Often the needs of the business "i.e. to grow and make profit" completely override the original purpose of an organisation. A company's focus can drift from fulfilling the functional needs of its customers. There are some classic examples, where long-standing brands/retailers that have fallen foul of this error; with catastrophic consequences.

Woolworths is probably one of the best-known examples in the UK in recent times. Known for children's clothes, pick and mix sweets and music singles (back when you purchased a physical copy). As customer behaviours evolved, rather than focus on their customer's needs, in the face of perceived competition from large out of town grocery chains, Woolworths tried to compete by expanding their range introducing kitchen wares and garden furniture. This for many customers diluted their purpose creating confusion. Whilst they dabbled with big box format stores with "Big-W"concept, this proved costly. They lost their purpose and connection with their customers, ultimately leading to their collapse.

Organisations start off filling a customer need or setting up in competition to be better or cheaper than the current offering. But many of these companies are built around fulfilling the business need. The older and more traditional businesses seem to struggle the most; such rigid hierarchical structures create barriers to customer focus.

Customer Experience is the "buzz word" of the moment, however, the true essence of being customer focused is being lost with mis-interpretation of what Customer Experience Management truly means.

*'Customer focus requires customer focus -
don't just pay lip-service - this takes effort.'*

Attempts to re-name functions and teams are, whilst well intentioned, not going to change the fundamental attitude and the behaviours required to enable a more Customer Focused organisation. By design such an approach inhibits the development of good intentions and can be damaging to the desired cultural outcomes. There needs to be a level of intentionality that is purposeful and centred around the customer and the employee. There will always be processes and therefore, performance measurement, but by organising the tasks and ownership of those functions, positive impact can be achieved.

To achieve the highest return on this approach, there needs to be an acceptance by everyone in the organisation that it is their responsibility to own the Customer agenda. At C-Suite Level there needs to be accountability for delivering performance against such functions.

Separate functional structures generate silos. Where there is Operations, Marketing, Brand and Insights all sitting separately there will be elements of the Customer Experience which are not managed through dissolved accountability. Whilst each stakeholder will have visibility of all the necessary tools and insights, by not being focused on the customer this ultimately ensures that the customer is never the primary focus and that no one is ultimately accountable.

A strong CEO will keep the customer top of the agenda, but it takes a brave CEO to change the structure of the business in order to embed customer focus.

Shifting the business focus whilst keeping pace with targets is not for the feint-hearted, but this can be achieved through planning and phased implementation.

Allowing the customer to be the primary focus of each business function creates departmental interplay which brings the biggest opportunity within customer experience.

A recent example is an organisation my company worked with to steer them through their contact centre transformation process. There were several parallel projects happening simultaneously which impacted the customer, in some way. However, all were governed by different departmental objectives. This was not deliberate, there was definitely positive intention. Yet, this company is not alone in focusing on the business outcome, not the customer outcome.

As a result, decisions were being made on the likely impact on the business, and not the impact on the customer. This was something we were determined to influence as we journeyed through their transformation.

To guide us we set a basic customer and employee framework adopting two simple checks by which each project decision was tested.

1. Will this make things EASY and add VALUE for our customers?
2. Will this make things EASY and add VALUE for our staff?

Consequently; focus was maintained on the customer, allowing us to move quickly onto new ideas in the evaluation phase, encouraging us to challenge why we did certain things, whether the reasons held up to scrutiny and whether the new thinking was likely to yield a better outcome for both staff and customers and, therefore, the business as a whole.

As with all good CX programmes, we started with a phase of Customer Journey Mapping. This was conducted as a multi-department exercise for a number of reasons. The first is obvious; to ensure that we have all the pieces of the jigsaw available to complete the picture. We were interested in sharing knowledge from each of the departments to understand what each function was, how it worked, and where each person in the room could improve the employee journey in delivering the customer experience.

The double benefit of this was to bring people together and get them thinking about how to improve the customer experience by making their own roles more efficient both for themselves but also their colleagues who were dependent on these functions and tasks. However, such processes run the risk of conversations happening in isolation of any data driven insights.

To mitigate this, the introduction of customer feedback was critical, but not just from the Satisfaction survey. This needed to be inclusive of other channels and more holistic.

"Insight without data is just opinion -
get into the detail to shape the big picture."

Reacting to feedback has to be taken both in context and with a degree of balance. A sample of one is purely anecdotal, an indicator maybe, but does not in itself make a solid platform for change.

Such indicators should not be ignored, but should be investigated further to understand their significance. This then allows you to make robust decisions with a higher degree of certainty and with more customer focus.

The measures typically available to organisations can be split into three listening posts:

1. Voice of Customer – Customer feedback surveys, focus groups

2. Voice of Employee – Employee surveys or discussion groups

3. Voice of Process - Business information, key performance indicator reports

The organisation we were working with, had no less than eight customer listening posts. Each of these was owned by a different department, providing different views and measures of the customer experience. Feedback from these listening posts was filtered and presented based on what the owner of the data wanted to share. As a result, linking the data to understand the *Why* on such insights was being missed.

The solution was to align the listening posts and to create a single view of the customer data. By building a repository for all touch-point data hosted in one single place, the business was able to create direct and personalized engagement. From fraud prevention, digital marketing preferences, to supporting customer care by showing their detailed order history.

*"Simplicity Of Purpose And Action
Leads To Organisational Buy-In."*

This is a long-term commitment and is a continuous journey of improvement. Not every adjustment needs to be a Paradigm Shift – small incremental changes are more easily accepted and adopted into every day behaviour.

We took an existing framework for customer service but evolved the processes in the background to make agents more accountable and allow them to engage better with both internal and external customers.

Developing this further, we have created the "ELASTIC" Customer Recovery Framework. This is geared to help businesses more easily adopt a more empowered customer focus in their contact centres.

E MPATHISE — Show empathy, believe and connect with the customer

L ISTEN — Shut Up! Listening will save effort and help you understand

A POLOGISE — Sorry is not guilt, but a human to human appreciation of the situation

S ORT — Sort the problem, customer contact is an opportunity to fix the issue

T HANK — Show gratitude and thank customers for sharing their experience

I NFORM — Inform customers of progress; remind them they are important to us

C LOSE — Give clear closure to the case when resolved in the eyes of the customer

"Leading with empathy and closing the loop to recover customers in crisis!"

The intention is to enable businesses to evolve from Customer Service to become a Customer Care team. For this to become adopted and truly embed itself into the business, we set clear boundaries. Without these boundaries Customer Service teams could revert to giving away the crown jewels just to close the case and get the customer off the phone.

The ideal from a business perspective of course, is to minimise loss. However, there are clear ways to do this which have a higher value to the customer yet are more cost efficient to the business.

To win the hearts and minds of all key stakeholders, it was important that we communicated the vision clearly and developed this collaboratively to ensure both relevance and universal buy-in. By creating a simple overarching plan that was revisited regularly, the processes and ambition of the project became embedded.

But this ambition had ground rules, after evaluation it was clear that there were significant internal barriers to change.

"I know what I like, and I like what I know."
Hackett, S. (1974) Genesis

Upon reflection with the group, these barriers were not as insurmountable as first thought. The perspective of the team and the fear of change being the greatest.

These basic ambitions created a pathway to a better solution, maintaining motivation of the group. Letting go of a task or function can be both daunting and liberating at the same time. Our role as CX professionals in this case is to give confidence and provide comfort to the change process.

The outline is demonstrated below in the seven project ambitions loop:

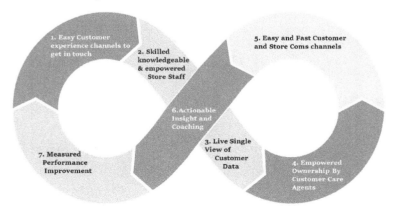

Underpinning this approach was a decision matrix. An action guide for certain situations that enable agents to have conversations with customers that are personal, efficient and actionable. This in turn created a much higher level of satisfaction, both for the customer and the agent. This simple and easy to follow approach can be rolled out beyond the contact centre through to the store level teams who engage with customers. This starts creating brand service consistency. Through managing customer expectations, we allow brand values to be demonstrated to both customers and staff!

As you embark on your CX transformation journey, remember the simple framework of this chapter:

1. Customer focus requires customer focus

2. Insight without data is just opinion

3. Act with purpose!

You will be making change happen faster than you think!

About Nick Lygo-Baker

Nick is a leading expert in operationalising customer insight and was listed in the top 25 CX professionals listed by CX Magazine. Both a Certified Customer Experience Professional and a Certified Member of the Market Research Society, Nick has been helping brands measure and improve their customer experience for almost 20 years.

Over the past decade he has held global leadership roles within some of the worlds' top Customer Research organisations. Nick founded Paradigm CX Ltd in 2018, providing a virtual-CXO solution with hands on guidance for organisations looking to improve their Customer Experience.

A millennial Retail graduate, Nick's experience covers a broad range of B2C and B2B industries (including Retail, Hospitality, Financial Services, Automotive and Public Sector) designing some of the most innovative and engaging Voice of Customer, Mystery Shopping and Employee Feedback Solutions.

Connect with Nick via the following channels:

LinkedIn: https://www.linkedin.com/in/nicklygobaker

Twitter: @CXParadigm

Facebook: https://www.facebook.com/ParadigmCXLtd

Website: https://www.paradigmcx.com/

Customer Experience 2

3. VoC Insights
And Understandings

Analyse and understand
your customer to drive change

Customer Experience 2

Feedback: The Inconvenient Truth – Responding To The Development Opportunity

Richard Jordan

Look around you… and I mean, really look around you.

It's impressive isn't it?

When you look around you…and I mean when you really look around you, whilst you'd be excused for the somewhat pained expression that 'really looking around you' creates, you'd also be forgiven for not really seeing anything exciting at all.

After all everything you looked at is everything you have chosen to surround yourself with and everything you have chosen to surround yourself with, is there by your design… literally. Let me explain.

Everything you saw and everything you didn't see, everything that exists and everything that has yet to exist, exists because of feedback and our response to it.

Now look again.

From the chair you're sat in, to the car you drive, from the falling rain to the mountains of Appalachia and from the smallest atom to the cheese sandwich you ate for lunch, everything exists because of feedback.

Whether Darwinian, creationist, existential, spiritualist or vegan, everything that exists, gives credit to the 'feedback loop'.

Take a simple wooden chair for example.

The wood it's made of grew in part thanks to the environment in which it was borne, but it's functionality, value, adaptability and evolution was shaped by responding to the stimulus it received (a Tree's growth is dependent on its response to nitrogen, carbon dioxide, water and sunlight) and only the trees which were the most responsive to stimulus and adaptive to their environment survived (albeit only to become a chair). In a similar iterative process of development, the material covering the chair was chosen by manufacturers in response to the feedback your ancestors provided and its structural integrity designed with thanks to an occasional sore bottom. The design of the very chair you are sat on has adapted to become the most efficient chair its potential allowed, but only after a long and sometimes uncomfortable, continual process of growth, feedback, development and improvement.

This virtuous and cyclical feedback loop of cause and effect, stimulus and response, input and output are present throughout every element of our existence and never more so than in our own development as customer experience advocates. We have striven to push, stretch, grow and against all odds, sought opportunities to adapt to our customers evolving needs, where stagnation, comfort and atrophy the antithesis of our competitors.

It is perhaps therefore most clearly evidenced within our ability to shift from developmental equilibrium to one of sought discomfort which has become our greatest achievement and our accomplishments in the field of customer experience, testament to our ability to seek the edge of our comfort zone and our breach into the uncomfortable unknown. One must only look at our individual and personal periods of spiritual, intellectual, emotional and physical growth to identify that comfort must be set aside if we are to break free of our constructed paradigms and our ability to deliver positive customer experiences directly influenced by our ability to respond to our customer's feedback.

As evidence of the dichotic link between growth and comfort, it is perhaps within this space of uncomfortable growth where strategies are created, goals are achieved and where meaningful customer experiences are developed; as it that limiting belief we have grown to understand our customer's needs, where we lose our competitive advantage. We might attempt to anticipate and create the environment by which positive customer experiences will flourish, but it is only through engaging with feedback and in our measured and outward response where the greatest opportunities for growth can be evidenced and interestingly, where our Customers actively seek to engage.

One might reasonably assume therefore, that it is understood by those at the forefront of the customer experience industry, that businesses whose culture welcomes customer feedback are the very businesses most suited to adapt to their customer's needs, but it is within these cultures where risk of apathy is greatest. Inviting feedback is simply not enough. We must encourage our customers to create the feedback we might consider inconvenient and we must seek out the uncomfortable truth, as it is here where change can flourish. Positive reinforcement of a negative stimulus, the receipt of the inconvenient truth and our response to these opportunities are the true conditions for growth - and our customers know it.

Our customers know better than anyone the power of a Tweet and its impact on a business's reputation and whilst sometimes inconvenient to hear, we must encourage and create the channels by which it can be delivered quickly and easily. If we are to grow, we must similarly create the culture which encourages our teams to deliver the service which pursues customer feedback, developing the conditions to stimulate our customers to speak out and to deliver the positive and negative feedback from which to respond. This symbiotic relationship between customers and customer service advisors and between feedback and response, is crucial if we are to create a positive experience for our customers, as failure to create the environment for growth leads directly to failure.

As customer experience advocates, our desire to engage with feedback must supersede our desire for comfort and convenience. We must actively promote in ourselves and our teams, that behaviour which seeks out the uncomfortable opportunities for growth and we must run headfirst towards the feedback we do not want to receive, as it is the feedback outside of our comfort zone which encourages growth and it is the times in which we feel we are on the very precipice of our comfort zones, where we will see our greatest potential as businesses and individuals.

The welcomed process of learning from feedback can and perhaps should be uncomfortable (at least to begin with!) and we should welcome the opportunities to hear the inconvenient truth, as it is in this opportunity in which we can develop the responses and strategies to grow. Identifying the uncomfortable opportunities and responding to feedback we did not want to receive, is the measure of a business responsive to their customers' needs and by extension those that do not, cannot survive.

By creating a culture where feedback is welcomed, we encourage the key to driving change, as change from within the closed feedback loop is limited, if it even exists at all.

Often, our businesses are guilty of creating the customer experience we expect our customers to welcome, incapable of identifying our own bias and lack of reactive objectivity. Creating a customer experience strategy which encourages negative feedback is a good place to begin and a successful customer centric culture should create, welcome, receive, manage and respond warmly to their customers observations, especially those which are less than complimentary.

Businesses would do well to ask what opportunities are being missed where the feedback was inconvenient to hear and where ease and comfort of achievement has stifled creativity and growth.

Akin to the manager who fosters positive working relationships within their team by engaging openly with their staff, your staff must in turn engage openly with your customers and promote the opportunity to review the businesses and advisor's performance. This continual and culturally driven advocacy of open dialogue between customers and staff, observation, review, feedback and response, is essential if your businesses and staff are to develop and evolve, as those who favour the alternate, risk loss of market reputation, or worse a loss of customers.

As a UK Taxi company once told this author and found to their peril, "... why would we want to hear from our customers ... WE decide our own standards of Customer Service!...", opportunity to review individual staff performance is key to creating the strategies for optimal performance as it is the individual Customer Service Advisors who are often the greatest advocates of a customer centric culture.

We simply cannot continue to create closed feedback loops, where customer reviews and posted observations, fall to the virtual waste ground. To evolve with an increasingly instant gratification culture, we must engage with technology and create the opportunities for feedback, as the businesses who embrace the digital feedback loop embrace the opportunity to change. Our use of technology and application of the digital feedback loop revolutionises our approach to responding to the customer's of tomorrow and it is inevitable that the businesses who embrace technological solutions to welcome their customers feedback, will be the most prepared to evolve.

After all, it is simply within our chosen response to feedback where opportunities to grow will be present and where survival of the fittest is measured.

Look around you and I mean really, look around you.

Are you responding to feedback?

About Richard Jordan

Richard Jordan is an internationally renowned Learning and Development Consultant, Customer Experience expert and Chief Executive of Raggit, the Feedback App; whose Mission Statement is to, "Improve Customer Service".

After a decade in the Royal Marine Commandos and whilst operating in some of the World's harshest environments, Richard identified the importance of empowering, enabling and encouraging people to use their voice for change and created a platform to deliver immediate improvements to the customer's experience.

A highly sought-after public speaker, Tech CEO of 2020 and Cultural Enablement coach, Richard is a keen mountaineer and Customer Services influencer.

Contacts and links

To connect with Richard and to follow his exciting journey;

Follow the Raggit App on Instagram, Facebook and Twitter:

@theraggitapp

Download the Raggit App from your App store today and review individual Customer Service Advisors, with Raggit – the Feedback App

How To Make "Voice of Customer" Your GameChanger

Stacy Sherman

Who are your favorite companies, and what makes you brand loyal? People typically answer this question based on how well a business understands and meets their needs. Buying decisions go way beyond price as we often pay a higher cost to shop at a particular place. Consider coffee, for example. Customers, including me, spend triple the price at Starbucks compared to other local coffee shops. Why would we pay more money on purpose? The reason is that the most reputable brands, like Starbucks, proactively LISTEN to customers and use feedback to deliver personalized experiences that exceed customer expectations.

Source: David Clarke Global Chief Experience Officer and Ron Kinghorn
US Consumer Markets Advisory Leader
PwC Future of Customer Experience Survey https://bit.ly/32qyBP

The best in class companies also care about employee views and empowers their staff to deliver customer excellence. Their competitive edge comes from humanizing business, and you can apply the same principles no matter where you work.

Three Ways To Differentiate Your Brand

1. Leverage the Voice of Customer (VoC) In Everything You Do

VoC is a valuable research method that enables you to understand the difference between customer expectations and how well you deliver what they need. Even if you believe there is no gap, your customer may think differently, and you must know that to adapt your strategies. Customer perception is YOUR reality.

Asking customers about their overall satisfaction level helps you gauge the likelihood of them continuing to purchase and recommend your products and services. Getting high-level feedback is good, but the magic happens when you dig deep into the customer journey. I highly recommend you ask customers to rate their experiences and provide comments about EVERY interaction point, commonly referred to as "moments of truth."

If you have not launched a business and do not have customers yet, then co-create a journey map with your target audiences (also referred to as personas). There are plenty of resources on the internet to guide you through the process, including my blog, DoingCXRight.com. My point is that getting feedback in the right way and at the right time is essential for business success.

Most people rely on surveys as their VoC source. While valuable, it must not be your only method of getting customer feedback.

Additional useful data comes from:

- Website contact forms
- Interviews (online and in-person)
- Social media
- Ratings and Reviews (on your site and external rating pages)
- Website visitor behavior analytics
- Customer Care Call Data
- Website Live Chat

I recommend aggregating and centralizing all VoC insights to understand your customers' views from a holistic perspective. It's a critical job function, so either assign the role in your organization to someone who has the right skill sets, or outsource the work.

2. Turn Voice of Customer Data Into Actionable Insights

Obtaining customer feedback and analyzing the data takes time, but it is well worth it. You can't possibly develop products, services, and market messages without understanding what your customers think and feel.

There are tools to help you compile, analyze, and prioritize data so that you know where to focus your improvement efforts. Some reputable time-saving platforms include Qualtrics, Medallia, Hubspot, Clarabridge, and more. They vary in capabilities and costs. If you have minimal or no budget, then start with manual methods of collecting customer feedback and using the data to inform your business decisions and changes.

3. Close The Loop With Customers

If you ask customers what they think, then inform them what actions you took because of their feedback. For example, if you lead a focus group to design a new product, follow up with participants to show what you created because of their input. Even better, offer a discount that is not available to the public to express appreciation. If you have a centralized survey team who calls customers, share recordings and notes with your sales teams so they can contact customers, rectify issues, and thank them, too.

The Game Changer

Top performing companies combine Voice of Employee (VoE) and Voice of Customer (VoC) as part of their decision-making process. Asking employees for feedback makes them feel heard and valued. And, when that happens, their commitment and engagement to deliver customer satisfaction increases. Happy employees fuel happy customers. That is the formula for Customer Experience (CX) success.

15 Best Practices

1. Ask employees for feedback as it serves as a valuable data source, but VoE must never replace VoC.

2. Respect customer intelligence. People know when companies are claiming to be customer-centric but are actually "checking a box."

3. Make the feedback process easy and convenient. Provide options such as calling, texting, or emailing.

4. Improve your customer journey based on both qualitative and quantitative data. A smile or frown by itself does not reveal much. Learn the "WHY" and "WHO" factors.

5. Thank people for their time in giving feedback. Inform what you'll do with their input. Communication and gratitude go a long way.

6. Actively listen. Do not sound like a robot or reading from a survey script.

7. Personalize your customer communications. You will gain better response rates.

8. Choose your questions wisely. If you don't ask correctly, you won't get actionable answers.

9. Capture feedback often. Customer and employee needs are changing rapidly.

10. Listen to what customers are saying across different channels. Improve experiences based on a 360 view.

11. Share feedback results with internal stakeholders. It helps drive a culture where everyone owns the customer experience.

12. Knowledge is power. Do not let the fear of responses be a reason you do not ask for feedback.

13. Assess satisfaction and establish benchmarks for year over year comparisons. You cannot fix what you do not measure.

14. Recruit and hire customer-centric individuals to achieve your CX mission. It's all about people!

15. Create a culture where EVERYONE owns CX and is accountable for customer excellence, not just leaders at the top.

Source: www.Ruby Newell-Legner

Remember

Proactively ask for feedback and use the insights to improve customer and employee experiences. Let them know of what changes occurred because of their input, as that is how you gain loyal brand advocates. On the contrary, if you do not follow CX best practices, people will switch to a competitor. According to PWC* research, "1 in 3 will leave a brand they love after just one bad experience, and 92% would completely abandon a company after two or three negative interactions." It costs a lot of time and resources to make up for one unhappy experience.

I can't say it enough. Customer Experience must be intentional and never an afterthought. Make sure you are NOT just TALKING about it but actually DOING CX RIGHT!

About Stacy Sherman

Stacy Sherman is a Customer Experience (CX) Leader, Strategist, Practitioner, and Digital Marketer based in the USA. She's known for humanizing business and differentiating brands beyond price. Stacy is currently the Director of Customer Experience and Employee Engagement at Schindler Elevator Corporation and previously led CX at Verizon. When Stacy's not at work, she's coaching, blogging, speaking, writing for Forbes, and Advising as CX Founding Board Member at several universities.

Stacy is on a mission to help connect people and inspire great authentic customer experiences fueled by motivated, happy employees. It is the reason she started DoingCXRight®, which is a journey-based framework that maximizes satisfaction through a practical approach. It entails both heart and science — combining proven methodologies to create real brand affinity, loyalty, and a competitive edge that delivers results. Learn more about Stacy and her CX mission to help people like you.

Visit Stacy Sherman's website:

www.DoingCXRight.com

Follow Stacy on Social Media:

Twitter.com/stacysherman

Linkedin.com/in/stacysherman

Instagram.com/doingcxright

People First - Why Should We Care?

Bruno Guimarães

I will start this chapter with a famous quote from Simon Sinek that summarises everything, and you should read it every morning, so you never forget about your people. The quote says:

"100% of customers are people. 100% of employees are people. If you don't understand people, you don't understand business."

Simon Sinek.

The statement is true for every kind of business which makes it even more powerful. Understanding the whole idea about putting people first is the start for any successful voice of customer (VOC) and voice of employee (VOE) program. I really don't believe that VOC works without a VOE or vice versa. They are two pieces of the same puzzle and combined, are highly effective. I am not saying that it's not possible to have a VOC program without the VOE, but it doesn't make a lot of sense because the front-line employees have valuable information about the customer that could change the whole company. If they don't have a voice, they will just keep the insights to themselves and keep doing their tasks just to finish another day of work.

People have dreams, they want to feel valuable, they want to be part of something, they want to be heard.

Implementing a VOC and VOE program takes time, effort and commitment. It looks simple, but it is a long-term journey to make it work efficiently. If done properly you will see a lot of quick wins that will help you to get c-level buy-in to the program and expand it to the entire company. But like I said, it's a long-term investment. Be sure to celebrate every small win, that will help get the spotlights to the program.

Once you start to listen to your employees, they will feel valuable and motivated because their opinion matters to the company. Job satisfaction will start to rise, and the company will have a team ready to make changes. Start small and take one step at a time. Remember it's a long-term journey. By starting small you will have more control of the program and of the people involved. But always have in mind that communication is a crucial part of the process. People need to understand where to go, understand the goal and objectives. Clarity will guide decisions about what data to collect. It's very important to know what questions you want to be answered, otherwise data will be just trash.

VOE and VOC can be a game changer. It can change culture, procedures and policies, employee attitudes and behaviour, and even the way company does business.

Challenges of Voice of Customer

We are living in an era of information, everything that we do is tracked somewhere. From your phone, Telco's have access to all the places you go - they have the exact location. In Brazil they are even using that data to understand the efficiency of social distancing during the pandemic period. They are tracking which regions people are respecting the stay home alert and take decisions based on those numbers. Facebook knows everything about you, from the things you like, to what kind of subject engages you, to a conversation or what kind of things you buy online. Watch the documentary 'Terms & Conditions' – then you will understand what I'm talking about. But be ready for it. Privacy is gone in the digital world. Social Media Today published an article from Irfan Ahmad, in June 2018 talking about the amount of data that is generated every day. It's shocking but it's true.

"Over 2.5 quintillion bytes of data are created every single day, and it's only going to grow from there. By 2020, it's estimated that 1.7MB of data will be created every second for every person on earth."

Thinking about clients, they are also creating a lot of information about the company, products and people. That information comes from all kind of sources, social networks, product reviews, surveys, customer service but they are all unstructured. One of the biggest challenges for the company is to structure all that information in order to start understanding the touchpoints and pain points of the client.

I always like to say that every single company has two sources of information that are treasure boxes. Complaints (customer feedback) and employee feedback. There is nothing better than complaints, every customer complaint is an opportunity to discover a better way of doing something, it's an opportunity for the company to understand their needs and wants. Complaints are genuine, a customer will not complaint just for the fun of it. He will do it because he has a problem and he wants a solution for it. If he is complaining, it is because he cares, he wants to be heard. Embrace it and start looking for solutions. The worst case is when a client doesn't complaint and just quits doing business with the company. You will never know what happened.

The Perfect World

Let's create a scenario here. Stay with me. You are the Customer Experience Manager, you get to your workstation, open your e-mail, and receive your customer feedback report from the last semester. You have all kind of information in it. Feedback is separated into clusters of types of problems, so you can understand what the pain points are very quickly. You have sentimental analysis from the feedback. Reviews, social listening and also answers from your NPS and CSAT surveys. Since its all structured and clustered it's very easy to understand the root cause of the problems, where the company is losing money, and prioritise which problem to attack first. Remember that attacking the most frequent problem it's not always the best option, you need to understand which problem has a higher impact in the business and in Customer Lifetime Value. From that point on you can map the journey, understand the pain points and design a new experience for your client. Once the company starts to understand the needs and wants of the customer and acting on the change, business will go to the next level.

If we tie to that employee feedback, then we have everything needed to change the culture and make the best customer centric company ever. Front line employees listen to customers every single day, they know the gaps of the process, they know what makes the customer mad, they know all the good and bad touchpoints delivered by the experience. For some reason, the managers do care about it, they are losing time and money producing all kinds of surveys. Before doing any survey, talk to the employees. Create a client war room to discuss real cases, to brainstorm new ideas, stimulating employees to talk. They will feel valued, they will believe they are part of something and that their jobs matter. Make sure to create a channel for them to constantly add feedback and ideas. Never forget to promote and reward the best ideas. That will give the confidence for all to change their attitude and behaviours and start to share insights. At the end of the day the employees will be engaged, happy to have a voice and ready to give the best experience they can to their clients. Treat employees as a valuable source of feedback. Engaged, loyal employees reduce costs, improve productivity and come up with more creative ideas.

It is very important and necessary that the employees get the right training and tools to work. They need to understand the company values and objectives, so they are all swimming on the same direction. Communication is key for a successful change. If your team have the right tools, the skills and understand where they need to go, they will deliver the results. Treat your employee as a client. Understand their journey, what are their pain points, what makes them motivated and what doesn't. Make them feel special. Alfred Lin, who used to be Zappos Chairman once said, "To have happy customers, we need happy employees. To have happy employees, we need a great company culture."

The Reality

Getting back to reality, the situation above is the ideal world for us as managers. But the truth is that on daily basis we don't get that beautiful report ready to make the decision. Here comes the real challenge of building a Voice of the Customer program. It takes a lot of work to sustain long-term commitment, but it pays off. Tackle one problem at a time, understand it, implement a solution and measure it. Everything needs to be measured and compared. What were the results after the implementation of the solution? Keep track, make sure you are going on the right direction. If not, adjust and measure it again. Those results are really important to get c-level buy-in into the program.

I would say that 90% of solutions to pain points are all on the customer feedback reviews - they will give all the information needed to make the change. Of course, it takes time to organise, it takes a lot of work, but with the right tools and team you can do it. Once you start you will never stop because it's a very open-minded experience. Processes and customer needs will become very clear and by the time you start mapping the customer journey it will be very easy to identify the pain points and design a new experience. Dig deep in customer and employee feedback. Always look for the root cause of the bad experience, understand what's working and what's not.

The main challenge is not finding the solution, but to understand and uncover the needs of the customer. You have the information, but it needs to be organised. It's a puzzle that you need to put the pieces in place, otherwise you won't have anything. Having huge amounts of data doesn't mean anything. If you don't ask the right question you won't have the answer you need. Share all the learnings from customer feedback, with the whole enterprise, everyone needs to know about it. The customer data can help fix problems, design new products and services, improve the customer journey, reduce cost and eliminate bad processes and policies.

In today's world the customer has the control, they have the power. Consumption and buying behaviour are changing like never before and companies need to understand the new customer. Products and services are all becoming the same, they are all commodities and fighting for price is not the best solution. What will be a game changer and will differentiate businesses are experiences. To deliver a great experience we need to understand what motivates, what are their wants and needs of the clients. The VOC and VOE will help extract the insights to change the mindset and transform the culture to deliver such an incredible experience. The customer will be willing to pay more and be happy about it. That should be the goal of every company.

About Bruno Guimarães

Bruno Guimarães is a Customer Experience Specialist certified by CX University, founder of the biggest CX community in Brazil called Amigos do CX, Co-founder of the first independent CX event in Brazil called Wow Summit and judge for the North American Customer Centricity Awards. Passionate about customer experience. Hands on, believes in collaborative learning. Extremely  curious about people, process and technology. On the free time he is a triathlete and marathon runner.

Contacts and links

https://www.linkedin.com/in/brunorguimaraes/

https://www.linkedin.com/company/amigos-do-cx/

https://www.instagram.com/amigosdocx/

4. CX Design And Improvement

**Creating experiences that engage
customers and employees alike**

Customer Experience 2

The Elephant In The Room

Betül Yılmaz

On the one hand we have advanced analytics, artificial intelligence, blockchain and robotics. Even space tourism is about to commence. On the other hand, customer-centricity is something most organisations in the world cannot achieve. Customer experience is not rocket science, but it is complicated, with 'people' being the unknown factor of the customer experience. In organisations, human beings work to create value for other humans.

A human-centred design tool solves this equation, with two unknowns, whether the process is well-managed, according to your organisation's dynamics and the people involved from each C-suites operational level. It encourages organisations to focus on the people they are creating for, which leads to better products, services, and internal processes[1]. The magic happens when enhancing value to customers and creating a continuous collaborative work environment.

---

1. From IDEO (https://www.ideou.com/blogs/inspiration/what-is-design-thinking) retrieved 04,June,2020

A Journey Starts

There is a parable from ancient India about a group of blind men and an animal unknown to them. By means of touch, each explored only a different part of the elephant's body. The first person, touching the trunk, said, "This being is like a thick snake". Another thought the ear was similar to a fan. A third exploring its leg, believed it to be like a tree-trunk. The fourth, touching the side, thought it was "a wall". A fifth man compared the tail to a rope, and the last, feeling the tusk, stated the elephant is hard, smooth and like a spear.

This parable has various endings, according to different sources. My favourite one is, "Each man touched only one part. Only when you put the parts together, you'll see the truth."

The Fact

Organisations aim to deliver functional, accessible, and emotional experiences for those they serve. Great experiences create loyalty and provide continuity. In reality it is not easy to achieve; two main reasons being organisational silos and not considering the final evaluator - the customer's entire journey.

Organisational silos view the truth according to their own expertise and experience. Their reality is 'a part of an elephant' instead of the whole. In order to grasp the big picture, we need to synergise cooperation, and gather combined expertise and experience, with one vision. Excellence in organisations requires meeting and exceeding customer's expectations on the entire journey. A sound voice and involvement of the customer points the way to new and improved experience initiatives.

Corner Stones

In order to achieve and manage a major improvement project in a big corporate company with strong silos and involve customers in this process, I will detail a best practice of managing the redesign of a customer journey, enabling teams to craft a successful human-centred design project, for organisations forging organisational silos working together, led by the customer's voice.

| Involve your people | Involve your customer | Use data | Communicate | Celebrate success | Project Journey |

1. C-Suite Buy-In

Each organisational department knows their part of the customer's journey, so we need interdepartmental involvement. Identify departments by mapping the internal stakeholders of your customer journey. Using an initial journey map, detailing each step of the customer journey, and including each departments' role or function areas they are responsible for, will help departments recognise their specific and the overall steps in the process. A stakeholder map assists cross-functional team project work. Visit each departmental C-suite, talking about your project, from sharing customer stories to prioritisation levels, getting their buy-in.

Explain your stakeholder map and ask the C-suite to identify appropriate members from their department. After your visits, divide the complete list of team members into two teams, ideally five to eight people in a team, focusing on cross-functionality. Inform the teams assigned, via email.

Remember, starting from the first step, to shoot photos, selfies and record small videos. Share them at the beginning of each meeting taking five minutes to talk about the project journey.

2. Sponsor And Advisory Board

Post C-suite interviews ask the most interested C-suite member to become the project sponsor. If the project is mainly about sales, avoid making the head of sales the sponsor, to avoid bias. Your sponsor will be your advocate in all decision-making meetings and thereafter.

Involve mid-level management, as the members of the advisory board, considering their decision-making abilities and vision. The latter will assist this project with their expertise and can decide on the swift execution of quick fixes of your findings, while the project is still ongoing.

3. The Initial Kick-Off And The Kick-Off Meetings

Prior to initial kick-off, final approval of the project objective and KPI's are obtained with the sponsor and the accountable C-suite members. In the initial kick-off meeting, introduce the project, KPI's and working method to the team. By request, the project sponsor delivers a motivational speech. We also organise a 'get-to-know' team workshop, and provide information about project methodology. Often team members, delivering an experience to the same clients are not familiar with each other.

All the C-suite members in the organisation and the advisory board are invited to the kick-off meeting, which introduces the project, objective and KPI's, using photos and videos of previous meetings. The sponsor and the C-suite members responsible for the project's budget, get a speaking opportunity, sharing their vision for the project.

Afterward, team members present their roles in this customer journey, propose and vote on project names. Finally, a customer shares an experience of their journey.

Finalising the first three steps in a week, we proceed with the following:

- Arrange a workplace for each team to work; a private meeting place where they can use the walls as a creative canvas, with sticky notes.

- Teamwork and confidence; with permission from direct reporters, allow for two project-focused days per week for team members. Empower the team, ensure your availability to accelerate the process. Set ground rules. No assumptions are allowed; we start from new and question every step. Celebrate the success after each turn.

- Agenda management ; stick to your agenda and don't drag out the project, as it can overwhelm the company. Set all meetings from the first day. Ask team members to inform in person those who couldn't attend about the outcomes. The ideal project time is six weeks. Hold an advisory team meeting each Friday, so project teams can report back. Schedule a C-suite meeting every 15 days, to report on outcomes and get feedback. This way, you will keep organisational levels informed and vocal, with no unexpected feedback at the project conclusion. Running a project for the first time, use your sponsor's authority to manage the agenda, which earns you that authority going forward.

- Communicate. Be innovative. Create a mascot bearing the name of the project, with mock-ups. Using them in all the C-suite meetings helps visualising your project. Leave mascots in meeting rooms so whoever has a meeting sees something different is happening. Leave notes on them. Invite people for a lean coffee to inform as many as possible about the project. Anyone in the organisation will notice and start talking about it. Write your progress updates on the mascots. During coffee breaks, people will start asking questions and contribute to your project.

- Use proper data for each step of your process making people understand its financial dimensions as well. Illustrate for example, how many customers were lost; or how time can be saved by changing a simple operation; the net promoter score and return of satisfied customers and their continued business with you.

4. During The Process

First week: Each member of the team must conduct at least one customer interview. Encourage the use of empathy and discovery maps, noting everything, and record all interviews with cameras or voice recordings. Direct half of each team to interview employees determining their experience while delivering the customer journey.

On the second day let them do the empathy map. Afterwards, let them present their findings to the advisory board. You will have a bunch of quick fixes from customer and employee interviews. Conducting the interviews, interviewers responsible for the back-office operations, will find quick fixes. Assign these to the advisory team for action.

Second week: It's time to reformulate the challenge, create personas and customer journey maps, and integrate one persona, based on discoveries made in the interviews, focusing on needs. The customer journey map visualises the current state, as experienced by customers. This enables you to identify improvement points and new opportunities. Let the teams reframe the problem again, and at the end of this week, present customer insights, empathy maps, personas and a journey maps with a longer list of quick fixes to C-suite members. Show videos as much as possible and play voice records of customer comments.

Third week: Facilitate the ideation session, inviting the advisory board and the teams. Inform attendees about possible technologies for solutions. Ask vendors to present cases. Encourage teams to openly generate as many ideas as possible. Do not kill, merge or criticise any idea. Visualise the ideas. Immediately organise another session with the C-suite, the advisory board and the teams, present the ideas and let them vote according to viability, usability and feasibility.

Fourth week: Prototype your solution and let the teams test with the customer. Actively listen, observe and note all reactions to your prototype. Use feedback for evaluating the test. If needed, revisit steps that you need to iterate.

Fifth week: You can redesign your future customer journey, after reaching your final solution. The rest is the planning and execution.

Coming To An End

Our first project was not easy, but after two projects, people requested help running their own projects, by involving the customers, or if they could contribute to our projects. They now understood the connection between departments' roles as a piece of a customer journey. Meeting customers made them more emphatic, while doing business as usual. The company gains a holistic viewpoint. Decision-making becomes integral to the project itself.

Each person involved in the process recognised that customer's driven solutions added value to their work, and they defined and eliminated non-essential procedures. More than 100 quick fixes were identified and fixed within the project time frame, with help of the advisory board.

The new journey rewards greater satisfaction and is appreciated by the customers, with high turnover.

About Betül Yılmaz

Betül Yılmaz is a customer experience consultant and founder of Elephant Istanbul, a customer experience and design consultancy company.

Betül has 17 years of broad range of banking experience, including customer experience, sales, marketing, business development and product development. She has managed projects across a wide range of disciplines: segment management, products to alternative delivery channel management, and reengineering projects.

She was offered the opportunity to work on an international start-up bank as Head of Sales and Marketing for five years. Her last position was at TEB - BNP Paribas Joint Venture in Turkey, as Head of Marketing and Customer Experience.

She is a professional executive coach, lean change agent, motivator a successful team builder.

Her passion is teaching clients where there is a will there is a way and discovering the right path reach magical corporate rewards.

To connect with Betül

Follow her on social:

https://www.linkedin.com/in/betul-yilmaz-2b48711a

Visit her web page:

https://www.elephantistanbul.com

Behavioural Science – The Importance Of Designing Customer Experiences With Humanity

Michelle Badenhorst

Many companies are struggling with the concept of identifying customer needs and expectations with a view to designing more customer centric products, services and ultimately experiences. There are many factors contributing to this but one of the most cited and widely acknowledged challenges is the fact that humans are mostly irrational in their decision making and they don't always know what influences their decision making. We often see that what people say they are going to do and what they actually do are not the same. This makes it tremendously difficult to design products, services and experiences based on what people say they want or need.

Consumers are people and are therefore emotional beings. They fall in love, they regret their choices, they do silly things and they even sometimes do things just to satisfy other people. At their core, human beings are impulsive and irrational. People typically form judgments or make choices based on the context around them, as opposed to Econs.

Dick Thaler and Cass Sunstein talk about Econs in their book, Nudge. They describe Econs as supernatural life forms that live in economic textbooks. They are super smart and forward looking and they have the ability to compute something called the 'utility of objects'. But most importantly, they always make perfect rational choices because they don't have emotions and they don't consider the context when making decisions. They have the ability to compute reasonably complex calculations without blinking an eye.

The best way to illustrate this point is by using one of the most relatable examples. Try to recall your last visit to your favourite coffee shop. Many of these outlets sell your favourite coffee in three sizes: small, medium and large. Think about what size you opted for. You will probably not find it surprising if I tell you that the most popular size of coffee anywhere in the world is the medium size.

Behavioural research has found that it doesn't actually matter how much coffee is in the medium cup, people will most likely choose the medium size because to their point, the large cup is too big and the small cup has too little, but the one in the middle has just the right amount of coffee. The outcome has been repeated even if the actual cup sizes has been increased. It also turns out that this phenomenon doesn't only apply to coffee.

This is a great example of the context effect – when people don't have an idea of how to value objects or calculate the 'utility of objects', they use information from other contexts to help them make decisions. The 'utility of objects' calculation refers to humans' ability to calculate the value of objects through the application of mental accounting processes. This reaffirms the role of context in human decision-making and just proves how predictably irrational human beings can be.

Short Introduction To Behavioural Science And Behavioural Economics

These are some of the interesting findings we can contribute to the field of behavioural science. This involves the study and exploration of human and animal behaviour through controlled, real-life observation and structured scientific experimentation. Behavioural studies rely on human subjective research to explain observed patterns of behaviour rather than quantitative data. It helps us to understand, predict and influence human behaviour in a meaningful way.

The Merriam Webster thesaurus defines behavioural science as "a branch of science (such as psychology, sociology, or anthropology) that deals primarily with human action and often seeks to generalise about human behaviour in society".

Behavioural economics unify ideas from economics and psychology and it mainly addresses the idea that individuals don't always behave rationally and don't always behave in their own best interest when it comes to making financial decisions.

Behavioural Economics Case Studies

Consumers have many payment options today; they can pay by cheque, cash, credit card, debit card, gift card, or even with their smartphones linked to mobile banking applications. Research has been done to see if the different payment methods could influence consumer perceptions of the brand and their products. Experts went further to assess whether there was a correlation between consumer payment choices and a likelihood to repeat purchases. They believed there was a fundamental cultural shift in consumer behaviour related to cash payments and brand loyalty but needed to test their hypothesis.

The research found that there might be a drawback to cashless convenience. It emerged from the data that psychological painful methods – like paying in cash - might be better in the long run because consumers feel more connected and more attached to the item purchased. It also increased the likelihood to repeat such purchases. The reason for this behaviour is because when individuals feel more connected, they become attached to products and don't dispose of them as quickly.

Hence, it might be more beneficial for companies vested in building long-term relationships to encourage cash payment methods more than plastic.

Benefits Of Integrating Behavioural Economics And Experience Design

Organisations can learn or borrow a lot from the field of behavioural studies and the decades of human behavioural research which mainly remains in academia, when it comes to redesigning products, services and finally customer experiences. Consumer behaviour helps brands understand what drives individuals and organisations to purchase certain products and support certain brands.

On the flip side, companies can also contribute to the existing research by becoming experimental organisations. Experimentation is a high-speed learning model and a huge source of insight on human behaviour and motivation. Both academic and business communities can benefit hugely from integrating some of the theories with practical methodologies.

Even though some organisations and business functions, like marketing, are already incorporating some of the behavioural research findings, there is much more to gain from integrating behavioural science more closely with experience design.

Many authors and design specialists, including myself, have noted the importance of considering the 'peak-end' rule when designing customer experiences. Daniel Kahnerman, author of Thinking, Fast and Slow explains that customers often remember their latest interaction with a brand, due to the cognitive memory bias, or the 'Peak-end effect'. Customers have selective memories when it comes to experiences and don't necessarily perceive the sum of their experience but rather how it was at its peak and how it ended.

These are just some of the behavioural insights we as customer experience professionals are currently tapping into when we redesign or optimise our brand experiences.

Behaviour-First Design

Joshua Porter of inspireUX cited: "As designers we must remember that behaviour comes first. We need to observe human behaviour if we are to support it in design." He feels very strongly that designs which support human behaviour will be more meaningful and successful. From this comes the notion of behaviour-first design. Behaviour-first design is about understanding the hidden factors that influence how people think and make decisions in a systemic way (see Consumer Behaviour Model below).

Behaviour-first design integrates various disciplines like psychology, design thinking, and various creative problem-solving methods to find out why people do what they do in order to figure out - through experimentation- what needs to change.

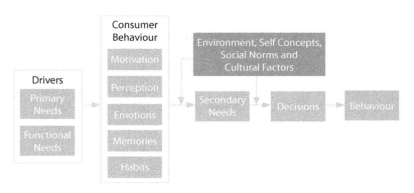

Amended Consumer Behaviour Model

Dan Ariely explained in the book Predictably Irrational some of the hidden forces that drives people to make decisions which are often far less rational than we would think. Only when we can really understand these influences can we design interventions that lead to meaningful change.

Key Behavioural Economics Theories To Incorporate Into Experience Design

Although behavioural science and economics have founded and documented vast amounts of findings and theories related to behavioural aspects, the following theories seem to be the most popular. It's a well-documented fact that the following four strategies can influence behavioural changes:

1. Restrictions and/or Constrains - businesses can effectively use restrictions or constrains to influence consumers to choose one product over another.

2. Incentives (both positive and negative) - businesses can use incentives to influence consumers to move from one product to another. They can use negative incentives to get consumers to stay with a specific product.

3. Market Persuasion – businesses use marketing and advertising information to influence consumers decisions.

4. Choice Architecture – method used by business to influence consumers' choices by "organising the context in which people make decisions". Nudging is a well-known choice architecture strategy.

Other behavioural science theories to consider when designing or redesigning experiences:

• Choice overload – the notion that too much choice can reduce sales conversation rates and that to many choices can create buyers' remorse which could lead to consumers regretting their purchase.

- Context effect – consumers are much more likely to base decisions on immediate contexts rather than calculating the value of the utility. This also means that customers' perceptions of value can be influenced by seemingly unrelated factors.

- Preference vocabulary - helps consumers to better understand and articulate their own personal preferences.

- Simplification - gives consumers less, simplified options to choose from.

Robert Cialdini synthesised years of psychology research in his book Influence: The Psychology of Persuasion. He introduced six principles of influence that help people persuade others. These six principles are reciprocity, consistency, social proof, liking, authority, and scarcity. Many organisations have subsequently incorporated these principles when designing products and services. These are explained in more detail below:

Robert Cialdini's Six Principles Of Influence

1. **Reciprocity** - Humans feel the need to pay back what they received from others. This can translate into free samples or generous discounts for consumers.

2. **Commitment & Consistency** - Humans tend to stick with what

they've already chosen and committed to. If consumers are already using your products or services, they are more likely to continue using them, which translates into brand loyalty.

3. **Social Proof** - Humans tend to trust more in the recommendations given to them by their social circles. If consumers demonstrate their satisfaction with a particular brand to their peers, they are more likely to buy into that brand as well.

4. **Authority** - Humans tend to follow people who seems like they know what they are doing. Here effective brand messaging is the key to converting new customers.

5. **Liking** - Humans are more likely to comply to requests from people they like. Here it's important to similarly target consumers to persuade potential customers to buy.

6. **Scarcity** - Humans tend to want what they cannot have or desire things that are exclusive and hard to come by. This involves creating strategies that will get consumers to act quickly and increases the likelihood that they will buy.

A good departure point is to use these theories as a foundation to develop and test our future state design while continuously looking for clues or mechanisms that drive people's behaviour. Start by asking the question: "How could we design products, services and experiences in such a way that they contribute to helping people achieve their goals or dreams?" Moreover, "How might we help consumers to make better buying decisions?"

The best designs will acknowledge what ordinary people aren't econs, but rather humans by building safeguards into their systems and experience. By doing this you will design environments that makes it easier for customers to make decisions.

Skills And Competencies Required

To successfully integrate behaviour-first design, organisations would need to make a mental shift. The best practice is to incorporate findings from academia as well as a behavioural science into your existing business design or development function. Organisations will need the following capabilities to achieve this:

- The ability to identify bottlenecks
- To foster an empirical culture that embraces trusted data and evidence-based decisions
- To use experiments to improve processes, products and services

Experience design, as we know it, will need a transformation. In order to successfully integrate behavioural science and experience design, you will need expertise in the following areas:

- Behavioural science
- Qualitative research
- Data analysis, and specifically statistical analysis
- Industry specific experience
- Project Management
- Communication
- Ethics
- Soft skills

Summary

Using behavioural sciences to uncover insights requires

a certain degree of humanity. You need to be willing to let go of your assumptions and ideas in order to make room for new insights. When designers understand the science and psychology behind human decision making and judgement, they become better designers because when they listen, they believe, and they become.

References:

- Wikipedia The Free Encyclopaedia, 'Behavioural Sciences', Wikipedia, https://en.wikipedia.org/wiki/Behavioural_sciences (accessed 28 May 2020).

- Merriam-Webster, 'Behavioural Science, Merriam-Webster, https://www.merriam-webster.com/dictionary/behavioral%20science (accessed 28 May 2020).

- Marc Schenker, 'How to use Cialdini's 6 Principles of Persuasion to Boost Conversations', CXL, https://cxl.com/blog/cialdinis-principles-persuasion/ (accessed 30 May 2020).

- Joshua Porter, 'Behaviour First, Design Second', Bokardo, 2009, http://bokardo.com/archives/behavior-first-design-second/ (accessed 30 May 2020).

- Astrid Groenewegen, 'What Is Behavioural Design?', SUE Behavioural Design, SUE Amsterdam & Behavioural Design Academy, https://suebehaviouraldesign.com/what-is-behavioural-design/ (accessed 30 May 2020).

- Polina Litreyeva, 'Top 5 features of consumer behaviour in e-commerce to increase your sales by up to 70%', Amasty Blog, 2019, https://amasty.com/blog/top-5-features-of-consumer-behavior-to-increase-your-sales/ (accessed 30 May 2020).

- Richard H. Thaler and Cass R. Sunstein, Nudge: Improving Decisions About Health, Wealth, and Happiness, New York, Penguin Books, 2009

About Michelle Badenhorst

Michelle is a hybrid design and business strategist that seeks to solve problems by applying various design methodologies and design mindsets. She is a passionate individual who enjoys helping courageous people to confidently inspire, initiate and implement meaningful change. As a business professional, she excels at helping businesses to drive real change based on customer insights, resulting in financial success.

Empathy and Customer Service are ingrained in her DNA. No matter where she goes, she easily spots opportunities and ideas to improve painful and frustrating customer and employee experiences. With her creative facilitation, design and product development skills, she has helped many organisations to improve and transform their businesses.

Michelle recently launched her own company, Map & Key.

Map & Key is a business consultancy that specialises in unlocking value to the business and their customers, through their unique Customer Experience Management offering. They integrate various business design methodologies and design mindsets, helping you to co-design and co-create purposeful business solutions.

Michelle very recently co-authored the first book in the Customer Experience series.

LinkedIn https://www.linkedin.com/in/michelle-badenhorst-70850783/

Instagram badenhorst.michelle

www.mapandkey.co.za

Treatment Of Customer Experience And Evolution To Omnichannel Customer Journeys

Patricia Sanchez Diaz

I am a strong advocate of the importance of identifying, understanding and operationalising customer emotions in any organisation. But I want to reflect on how organisations are now revisiting their business design to organise themselves around their customers via the management of the total customer lifecycle architecture.

It's a fundamental transformation but not an easy concept to deploy.

To operationalise this concept, an organisation definitely needs to set up dedicated teams to look after omnichannel end-to-end customer journeys; and to collectively own the holistic current and future state of their architecture blueprint.

These teams need to be highly accountable for the design and implementation of activities that ensure delivery of customer needs and outcomes.

The table below illustrates some symbols of change towards omnichannel end-to-end journey orchestration:

Construct of the team	Functional	Cross-functional	Multi-disciplinary
Ways of working	Waterfall	WAgile	Agile
Positional authority (Decisions)	Limited	Limited	Yes
Clarity of CX strategy (Purpose and Goal)	Limited	Limited	Yes
Framework (Customer life cycle)	Maybe	Partial or Yes	Yes
Treatment of framework	Continuous improvement	Design improvement	Service design optimisation
Scope focus	Offline	Online	Omnichannel

I want to explain some key reflections that relate to creating enlightened ominchannel end-to-end customer journeys.

My first reflection relates to organisations - that whilst driven by commercial targets - really do want to put customers are at core of what they do; that believe in customer centricity; and understand the importance of delivering the Brand promise to customers.

To deliver against the brand promise they set up customer experience teams tasked with creating a customer experience vision, a comprehensive program and a roadmap of projects and programs to deliver the best experiences for the customer.

Making this task a reality, however, might be challenging due to:

1. Business design and operating model. In many occasions these organisation's business design is a matrix of functions and divisions that build road maps and change plans based on their

individual objectives and goals. The business governance is based on multiple steering groups and committees typically operating waterfall. It is a silo operating model that prevents a "connected experience".

2. Positional authority. It is likely that the team has limited ability to make decision party influenced by the lack of meaningful budgets. They might rely on influencing projects and programmes. Their ability to drive change across the end-to-end journey is therefore inherently limited.

3. Understanding the customer purpose. The business design ultimately hasn't been created around the customer purpose or need. Data and Insights is gathered and used to support decisions but does not provide the overarching clarity on where the value lies for the customer. As an example, having an Net Promoter Score (NPS) program doesn't mean you are listening to your customers.

4. Understanding your business ecosystem. There is no holistic and comprehensive view on how processes, technology, people and systems collectively support the fulfilment of customer needs. In fact, there might not even be an awareness of internal complexities and how remote people's roles are from the customer purpose.

5. Metrics system. Customer metric typically is restricted to NPS or CSAT to which senior leaders and head of teams consistently look at; but in fact, customer- business and operating metrics are not often linked to each other, and the company has not yet stabilised a causal model between them. Again, this means they cannot really focus on what really drives value. Value to the customer (the experience) and value to the business (the money).

The outcome is a disjointed customer experience designed by disconnected silos.

CX teams' ability to drive substantial change is limited in

most cases to support change in growth or run and continuous improvement but is almost likely they are playing the "Whack-a-Mole" game - as soon as one problem gets resolved, another issue raises its head!

My second reflection relates to customer-led organisations that are driven by commercial targets, that have decided to drive most interactions digitally.

The CX team still is tasked with creating a customer experience vision, a comprehensive program and a roadmap of projects and programs to deliver the best experiences for the customer. The business also setup digital product teams to own the end-to-end digital customer journey.

Many of the challenges previously articulated still exist but with a twist, and I reflect on two challenges:

1. **Business design and operating model.** Like the previous one, but with the caveat that one of those programs might be called Digital Transformation. The organisation becomes "Wagile". The business ways of working are a hybrid between cross-functionality and multidisciplinary. The digital team is multidisciplinary shaped often by roles like: scrum master, product owner, UX, front end and back end developers, solutions architects, business analysts. They sometimes don't have as part of that core team roles such as: CX, service designer, researcher & insights, process designers, tech specialist, proposition designer, marketing or your customer facing team. These roles are often considered stakeholders or subject matter experts brought to the team to co-create when needed. But can you see the flaw? Digital teams use human centric design to deliver iterative improvements in their digital journey, yet most of the roles relate to implementation of change and not necessarily to understand the full end to end journey or your customer lifecycle architecture. By the way, I am not saying that all those roles need to be part of a core team, I am saying there needs to be a thought

around the roles that design and the roles that implement and which ones are really needed to create experiences and to deliver end to end experiences

2. **Positional authority.** There are many reasons as to why there is greater ability to drive positive change but still that won't be across the full end-to-end journey. And the digital journey is often misaligned with the offline or physical experience, primarily because they don't have control over the offline setup, E.g. retail stores, contact centre or engineers.

What digital transformation has brought is a customer-led model that uses human centre design techniques, innovates fast, creates concepts fast and delivers them to the customers fast. And a new way of learning about the customer and adapting fast to customers' expectations.

These digital teams can really be considered customer journey teams with the caveat that only look after digital journeys and not the whole end to end customer journey across all channels.

So once again, you might be playing "Whack a Mole".

My third reflection relates to companies seeking to create a connected experience across the organisation. They are putting in place a macro framework to answer one fundamental question: *If I only have one pound to invest, where do I invest it?* – The answer is where it provides most value to the customer (Experience) and the organisation (commercials).

Some components of that framework are:

1. **Customer framework.** They are using their customer lifecycle architecture as their main framework and consider journey management from a holistic point of view, to ensure the end to end customer experience is innovative, commercial, consistent and coherent across brand/s. Their customer lifecycle architecture is what I can only call the macro blueprint. One that

shows the orchestration of all customer journeys, their synergies and dependencies.

2. **Omnichannel customer journey teams.** They are setting up teams to collectively orchestrate the macro Blueprint. One that contains a comprehensive view of the above and below the line of visibility of all end to end customer journeys permitting to ascertain the health of all the journeys collectively. As if you were a doctor, it allows you to really understand where and why the symptoms manifest, where and why they originate. They are looking at the above and below the line of visibility, processes, systems, technology, demand flows, customer experience, expectations, tolerances, emotions, employee experience, across all channels.

3. **Service design.** They are implementing service design at scale, as an instrument to understand in detail their current estate and their future estate blueprint. In my view the best way to create a comprehensive "customer led" roadmap and backlogs of activities that mitigate current pain points and work towards a future estate in the medium and long term.

4. **Product design.** These organisations use customer led human centric design to ensure their propositions and products fulfil the customer need. They go one step further safeguarding that those propositions make sense in the context of the full end to end customer journey which in practice means commercial and customer teams working together as the norm guaranteeing customer outcomes are met.

5. **Agile at scale.** They are setting up agile at scale because contrary to what might look from the outside, Agile brings to teams' rigour, control and a realistic way to achieve targets.

6. **Macro framework.** Because having a customer framework is not enough, they are looking at putting a macro framework in place that truly ensures a customer led decision making, prioritisation and funding allocation, in the short, medium and long term for the organisation becomes the norm.

If your business is at this point, consider answering these questions:

- How do I setup at macro level the service design framework and the product design framework that delivers the brand promise and a compelling reason for customers to buy and experience your services?

- Are my back end and front-end systems able to support the macro framework?

- Are data and insights built to support 1) understanding your customer 2) understanding your end to end customer journeys 3) decision making, prioritising and funding?

- How to I align the experience across the touchpoints and interconnect them for the online and customer facing roles?

At this time, you might have stopped playing "Whack a Mole" and you are working towards a connected experience that delivers value to the customer and the organisation, you know exactly where the value lies and where to invest your money to obtain best returns.

I am inclined to think that in the next two to five years we will start seeing the rise of companies organising around my customer lifecycle architecture and setting up end-to-end omnichannel customer journey teams.

While omnichannel end-to-end customer journeys are optimum; and holistic customer centricity is admirable, especially it if ticks the commercial boxes, as I stated, it's a fundamental transformation but loaded with complexity and not an easy concept to deploy.

That said, it is highly prized and therefore why companies are in hot pursuit.

Patricia Sanchez Diaz

Patricia Sanchez Diaz is a certified customer experience professional (CCXP), accredited emotive CX practitioner (ECXP) and member of the customer experience professional association (CXPA).

Patricia is a regular speaker and awards judge, co-author of the first book: Customer Experience and Finalist at the My Customer CX Leader of the Year International Awards 2019.

Patricia has managed the full customer and product/service lifecycle and its architecture across a wide range of industries. Her expertise is within business customer experience transformation and strategy which includes service design implementations across omnichannel customer journeys.

However, her passion lays within human centricity, customers and employees alike, which has guided her to design an Emotions management framework; a tool to maximise business value and customer loyalty.

LinkedIn: linkedin.com/in/patriciasanchezdiaz

5. CX Metrics, Measurement And ROI

Using feedback and metrics to better understand commercial results

Dollars And Sense: The Cost Of Quality In Customer Experiences

Alec Dalton

In the mathematics of business, there is no equation more central than the basic profit formula.

$$Revenue - Cost = Profit$$

Within the field of customer experience management, attempts at monetising CX efforts often emphasise the first variable. Revenue, after all, is the direct financial contribution from customers to the businesses they patron. Metrics like customer lifetime value, annual recurring revenue, and marketing return-on-investment certainly have their merits for evaluating the impact of CX on sales, but financial partners are often distracted from seeing the true results of CX investments: traditional metrics like these can be rife with everything from the unpredictability of future purchases to convoluted calculations that rely heavily on estimation (or – worse – guesstimation!).

How else might you gauge the value of successful CX? Look instead to the cost variable, and more specifically to a concept called the *cost of quality*. This operations management framework conveys the hard costs associated with both poor customer experiences and the activities intended to thwart defective products and services. In other words, the cost of quality accounts for the expenses a business incurs when operating and combatting bad CX.

Consider this sobering fact from the American Society for Quality: many organisations miss 15-20% of their revenue trickling to the bottom line because of quality-related costs.[1] While some of these costs are necessary for ensuring satisfying products and services reach customers, many of these costs are equally tied to dissatisfying customer experiences and underperforming operations. Now imagine how useful knowledge of these costs can be when seeking CX investments: executives considering whether to finance such initiatives would almost certainly respond favourably to business cases that balance greater profitability with improved customer experiences.

Calculating the Cost of Quality

The cost of quality really represents the sum of four cost categories, first identified by Armand Feigenbaum.[2] The two most obvious categories are referred to as the "costs of non-conformance" or the "costs of poor quality," aptly named because these expenses result from defective products and services. According to Dr. Joseph DeFeo, Chairman of the quality-theorising Juran Institute, "The cost of poor quality provides proof of why changes must be made."[3]

External failure costs: Most pertinent to CX, this first category encompasses costs that arise after a product or service reaches the customer. Examples include:

- Repairs and related servicing;
- Product replacement or service replication;
- Refunds and rebate redemptions;

- Faulty product liability claims and legal redress;

- Complaint handling and resolution; and,

- Reputational damage, including negative word-of-mouth and the missed opportunity for positive referrals and repurchase.

In principle, all of these costs can be avoided if products and services perfectly match the requirements and expectations of customers. When problems do arise, it is possible for these costs to escalate, such as when poor complaint handling snowballs into secondary customer service issues.

Internal failure costs: Expenses in the second category arise when a defect is identified before the product or service reaches the customer. Examples include:

- Mistakes resulting in wasted resources and scrap;

- Rework when production needs to be redone;

- Breakdowns in production systems, plus resulting downtime;

- Inefficiencies that otherwise result in the waste of time and materials; and,

- Variations and inconsistencies in non-conforming output.

The Ritz-Carlton Hotel Company, known for offering high-quality luxury hospitality, personifies these costs with the playful acronym "MR. BIV;" employees are trained to recognize the enemy of quality before guests have the misfortune of meeting him![4]

Whereas the two types of failure costs occur when things go wrong, the opposing "costs of conformance" or "costs of good quality" are intended to ensure quality customer experiences. They might better be described as CX investments than costs.

Appraisal costs: Activities in this cost category are intended to identify defects throughout supply chains and production systems. Examples include:

- Evaluations of suppliers and incoming supply inventories to ensure quality inputs;
- Inspection, testing, and auditing measures for evaluating the conformance of work-in-progress or finished goods; and,
- Calibration of inspection tools and methods, intended to drive the consistent and accurate measurement of quality.

These activities are commonly addressed with the business function of quality assurance.

Prevention costs: The final expense category actually covers some of the first activities for achieving good quality. Examples include:

- Product and service design activities focused on achieving "inbuilt quality" in the fundamental requirements or specifications for products, services, and their supporting production processes;
- Training of staff on the avoidance and correction of human and mechanical errors;
- Fool-proofing techniques that automatically prevent or correct defective work-in-progress; and
- Quality planning efforts to continuously improve production processes.

As the name suggests, these costs are absorbed when trying to prevent defects from moving further along the production process and reaching the customer.

Reading these categories and examples, you likely considered instances where these costs arise in your own organisation.

As stated at the onset, the beauty of the cost of quality framework is that it can quantify customer experience and quality efforts in real monetary terms. With estimates for each of the cost categories, you could even calculate a holistic cost of quality:

Components of the Total Cost of Quality

Considering an Optimal Cost of Quality

At first glance, the cost of quality equation may cause concern: won't adding all these expenses produce an outrageous sum in order to truly achieve good-quality customer experiences? Fortunately, you can take a sigh of relief! The failure costs should actually occur inversely with the appraisal and prevention costs. Look at the following graph to see this relationship.

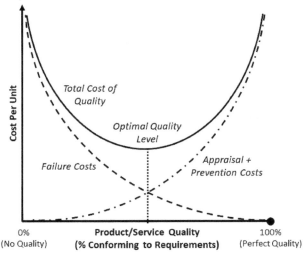

Adapted from Juran, J. M., & Gryna, F. M. (1988). Quality Control Handbook (4th ed.). New York, NY: McGraw-Hill.[5]

The scenario toward the left of the graph reflects what happens when there is no investment in quality operations and CX: failure costs skyrocket. The opposite occurs on the right side of the graph: while products and services function perfectly and achieve excellent experiences, the costs of appraisal and prevention are astronomical. Toward the middle, the costs of failure exactly equal the costs of appraisal plus appraisal. This trough represents the lowest possible cost of quality – the optimal cost companies should pursue to maximise profitability.

Containing The Cost of Quality with Customer Experience Management

As with any measurement in business, cost of quality numbers accomplish nothing unless subsequent action is taken. To achieve the optimal quality level, CX professionals and their colleagues across the organisation should partner to identify opportunities for reducing external and internal failure costs. Thought should concurrently be given to improving the appraisal of quality and the prevention of defects. The operations and quality management disciplines offer extensive methods and philosophies for addressing both concerns, with popular techniques including Six Sigma and Lean. The following simplified process captures the essence of many of these techniques and can easily be applied in CX operations:

1. Outline likely quality-related costs associated with the execution of your product, service, and experiential offerings. Review the four cost of quality categories to help organise the wide variety of expenses.

2. Review financial records to determine costs. Partner with colleagues across your organisation to calculate true costs or develop informed estimates.

3. Set a target for cost containment. In consultation with executives, especially those in financial and operations roles, consider

realistic goals for approaching the optimal quality level with the lowest cost of quality.

4.   Identify opportunities to pursue the target. Scan business processes and explore different areas where better appraisal and prevention measures can help reduce internal and external failure costs. CX professionals will find some of the most valuable insights coming from the voices of customers and employees.

5.   Contain costs and continuously improve. Implement some ideas and innovate business processes and product or service designs. Use feedback to continuously iterate and improve as you pursue the target.

It should be clear at this point that the cost of quality framework offers many benefits for customer experience management. First, it outlines the quality-related investment activities and failure costs arising from the delivery of products and services. Second, it quantifies an optimal quality level and total cost, which balance the investments versus the failure costs. Third, and most holistically, it offers a model for achieving increased profitability through cost containment. The cost of quality framework truly makes dollars and sense.

References

1. Cost of Quality (COQ). (n.d.). Retrieved June 12, 2020, from https://asq.org/quality-resources/cost-of-quality

2. Feigenbaum, A. V. (1956, November/December). Total Quality Control. Harvard Business Review, 34(6), 93-101.

3. DeFeo, J. A. (2001, May). The Tip of the Iceberg. Quality Progress, 34(5), 29-37.

4. Solomon, M. (2015, January 18). Eliminate Customer Service Defects With Ritz-Carlton's Simple System. Retrieved June 12, 2020, from https://www.forbes.com/sites/micahsolomon/2015/01/18/learn-ritz-carltons-simple-system-for-eliminating-customer-service-defects/

5. Juran, J. M., & Gryna, F. M. (1988). Quality Control Handbook (4th ed.). New York, NY: McGraw-Hill.

About Alec Dalton

Alec N. Dalton, CRDE, CHIA is a service scientist specialising in customer experience management and hospitality operations. He currently serves as Senior Manager of Global Quality for Marriott International, improving worldwide guest experiences while maintaining on-strategy hotels across 30 leading brands. Alec also serves as an Advisory Board Member of  HorizonCX, a boutique customer experience consultancy. He previously operated luxury hotels for The Ritz-Carlton Hotel Company and Walt Disney Parks & Resorts. In 2018, Hotel Management Magazine named him to the "30 Under 30" list of rising hospitality leaders. Alec's frequent writings include co-authorship of Customer Experience, the international best-seller preceding this book.

Contacts and Links

Website: AlecDalton.com

LinkedIn: LinkedIn.com/in/AlecDalton

Twitter: Twitter.com/AlecNDalton

The Business Acumen That Every CX Leader Needs To Develop

Janelle Mansfield

As a CX practitioner or leader do you struggle to get the buy-in and alignment you need from your cross-functional colleagues or leadership team? If so, it may be because you're not translating your knowledge and CX know-how into tangible results and terms that your colleagues connect with.

In this chapter we will dive into the key business concepts that will help you as a CX leader solicit and secure the support needed to drive Customer Experience initiatives forward in your organisation.

It's Important For All Leaders In An Organisation To Be Comfortable With Core Business Concepts

As CX professionals we are great at putting ourselves in the shoes of the customers, of understanding their journey and what's most important to them. However, there are many of us who are not so great at doing that with our cross-functional colleagues. Many CX professionals have progressed through the Customer Service ranks and have therefore not always been exposed to some of the other critical elements of business.

When you think of a business and its business model there are the following core key considerations as defined in The Business Model Canvas:

- Key Partners

- Key Activities

- Key Resources & Employees

- Value Proposition

- Customer Relationships

- Channels

- Customer Segments

- Cost Structure

- Revenue Streams

As a CX leader, if you aren't already able to describe, understand and align on those key considerations I suggest spending time getting acquainted with those concepts, and clarity on what those look like in your business.

For more information, and to download The Business Model Canvas go to *www.strategyzer.com*. I encourage you to get comfortable with it and add it to your CX toolkit.

It's Our Job As CXers To Help Our Cross-Functional Colleagues Be Successful

Some of the most successful CX practitioners in the business have this core characteristic in common - they always let others shine. While it's important to celebrate the successes of your team, it's even more important to help the rest of the business succeed as it's the reason the CX team exists in the first place. I suggest spending time getting to know your colleagues, what they're measured on, what makes them successful and what keeps them up at night. To keep track of this information dive into your CX toolkit and pull out your empathy map, fill it in for each of your cross-functional colleagues. Make sure to capture both what's core to their functional role, but also what's most important to them as a person.

Think Beyond The Customer

It might sound counterintuitive to suggest that as CXers we need to think beyond the customer, but we do. We need to be strategic in how we position ourselves and our initiatives within the company. If your company doesn't have a business case template that is used to seek approval for projects, create one. And, if your company does have one, review it to ensure that it captures core Customer related questions, like Impact on the Customer, Communications Required for the Customer, etc. More than that, use it. Use that business case template** for every single initiative. Be the champions for proper documentation. Provide regular and concrete updates to key stakeholders. And, most importantly, talk in numbers.

Numbers Are The Only Language That Matters

There's been much debate about the role that CX will continue to play beyond 2020, and ultimately it comes down to the Return on Investment that's being created. As CXers it can be hard to put down our accomplishments in something that's so black and white. Especially something that's as impersonal as a number. Regardless, one of the key reasons why businesses exist is to generate a profit. And, for us to succeed we need to speak the language of business: *numbers*.

Arm yourself and your team with this formula from Harley Manning of Forrester*:

1. "We propose to do A ...

2. ... to improve B ...

3. ... which will bring us economic benefit C ...

4. ... at a cost of D."

For example: "*We propose to redesign our B2B customer service portal to make it easier for our clients to fix their own tech problems which will save us $50 million per year by avoiding road trips by our tech support teams at a cost of $1.5 million.*"

CX Initiatives Must Quantify The Financial Benefit

Business leaders care about either top line growth (revenue) or the bottom line (revenue - costs = profit). Each and every CX initiative must be able to deliver either incremental revenue (or revenue protection) or a reduction in costs (cost containment /cost avoidance).

I am often told by clients that their organisations aren't mature enough and do not track data or generate reports on the financial benefit. My response is: "Just because they don't track it, doesn't mean there isn't a benefit. It just means your job is a little more difficult".

If you don't have access to the data you need to be able to report on a financial outcome for one of your projects, you will need to do some research. Think of it like a puzzle that you're trying to solve. Leverage whatever KPIs your company has, look for any internal information you have that can be extrapolated, seek industry benchmarks, consider your competitive intelligence to make assumptions. When using this approach** ensure you state your assumptions.

Know What Your Competitors Are Doing

In an organisation competitive intelligence often sits within the Marketing or Strategy functions, however it doesn't usually consider the customer experience. Therefore, it is also important to consider the competitive landscape from a CX perspective.

Many CX teams either complete a competitive assessment themselves annually or outsource it to a consulting agency. I recommend to my clients that this needs to be a core activity of any CX program, and it should reside in-house.

In all likelihood your customers engage with your competitors in one way or another, and those interactions shape and inform their expectations of their experience with you.

To make this feasible, consider assigning one competitor to each of your team members. Have them dedicate up to half a day per month on monitoring the experience being delivered through as many channels as possible. Create a standard template** for each team member to use to give structure and consistency to the assignment. Build into your regular team meetings a sharing opportunity whereby you cycle through a competitor at each meeting.

Leaders, particularly the C-Suite, are very concerned about what is happening in the competitive landscape, and are likely not well informed about the experience the competitors are delivering. This will allow you to always be ready to speak to what your competitors are doing, what changes they are making, where there may be opportunities and how your customers may or may not react, respond or be impacted.

Consider The Authority Levers

Finally, now that you're armed with the ability to understand and empathise with your colleagues, speak the language of business, respond to financial considerations and share competitive insights you are ready to start considering the Authority Levers that exist within your organisation.

Prior to bringing forward any business case, or sharing the results of a project, consider who in the organisation is most impacted, and who has the right authority to support your initiative.

There's strength in numbers, and having pre-alignment with key influencers beforehand can help get you over the finish line.

I remember I was once asked to complete a business case to assess the feasibility of a project that was near and dear to the heart of the CEO. After having completed the work I realized that my recommendation would likely be difficult for him to hear. With that in mind, I consulted his trusted advisor, the CFO. Getting him on board made breaking the news so much easier, and resulted in my recommendation being accepted.

In Summary

To help you succeed as a CX leader prioritise the following:

- Getting comfortable with core business concepts
- Acquaint yourself with the company's goals, measurable targets and priorities
- Consider what will help your cross-functional colleagues be successful
- Be strategic and business minded, by thinking beyond the customer
- Speak the universal language of business; financial outcomes
- Quantify the financial benefit of CX initiatives
- Shine through sharing competitive insights
- Leverage internal influencers

Remember, it's our job as CX leaders to speak the language and connect our competencies to those of our internal stakeholders. If we do the heavy lifting by translating our priorities into concepts they understand, like revenue growth or cost savings, we will all be further ahead, both in our own organisations and in the discipline of Customer Experience.

- *The One Sentence Business Case, by Harley Manning, Dec 2019, Forrester.com

- **Visit *www.amplifiedcx.com/learning* for access to templates and supporting articles

About Janelle Mansfield

Janelle Mansfield has an MBA that she has leveraged to support her clients in understanding the business side of Customer Experience. She is an experienced executive and management consultant in the disciplines of customer experience, marketing, communications, change management and strategy.

She is an early-adopter of technologies that foster better collaboration and engagement with customers, employees and stakeholders. Her previous corporate and client-focused experience has elevated the business results and practices of leading companies in multiple industries, including IBM Canada, Canada Post, the University of Ottawa, and Federated Co-operatives Ltd.

Janelle is a 3-time best-selling co-author of books on the topics of Leadership, Customer Experience and Remote Working. Customer Experience 2 is her fourth collaboration.

Currently, Janelle lives her purpose and passion by helping leaders amplify their customer experiences for better business results through her consultancy, Amplified Customer Experience (*www.amplifiedcx.com*).

To find out how to best leverage the principles discussed in this chapter, contact Janelle at *janelle@amplifiedcx.com* for a complimentary coaching session.

Or, connect with her on LinkedIn (include the note: "CX2" in your connection request): *https://www.linkedin.com/in/janellemansfield*

She also has video tutorials available on her YouTube channel: *https://bit.ly/AmplifiedCXYT*

What Really Matters Most To Customers?

Christopher Brooks

Do you know what matters most to your customers? Or is this the holy grail in customer experience? If you know what matters most to your customers, you can prioritise your resources to deliver the greatest value for your ideal customers.

If it is that simple why don't you pursue the concept? Is it because there isn't a recognised way to measure what matters most? Or is it because such an approach is difficult to work with?

In this chapter, I'll share how you can achieve this CX goal by introducing you to key behavioural change drivers. I explain how they are reliable, accountable and with a little application, straightforward to work with in CX management.

Key behavioural change driver analysis (or key buyer factors as they are sometimes called) is the study of identifying what experiences change customer behaviour. This approach is often overlooked when referring to the standard set of 'satisfaction', 'recommendation' and 'effort' measures. However, many vanguard brands in customer experience already use key behavioural change analysis to understand what really matters to their customers and have done so for several years.

The Importance Of Metrics In Customer Experience

CX, like any discipline, must be accountable to be trusted at the most senior levels within an organisation. You need to justify the value of your contribution. Conventional CX measures often leave practitioners frustrated because they are not reliant on the customer experience alone.

For example, if a company puts its prices up, or the press attack the sector in general, recommendation scores go down. However, neither of these reasons are because of a drop in customer experience quality.

This can lead to the focus switching from the customer feedback commentary provided alongside the scores to explain customer's views. Whilst you certainly should be reviewing why customers do or don't value experiences, if the original question is wrong how confident can you be the response is relevant?

One strength of key behavioural drivers is they are measures of actual change, based on activities which happen to your customer. There is a cause and an effect. The customer changed their behaviour because you delivered an experience.

In contrast, a customer's statement that they will recommend you may or may not be acted upon. It is inferred. Unless each intended recommendation is tracked, using codes, it is not possible to connect this to sales or any other business performance measures.

Without linking CX to business KPIs, the value of customer experience to the business is compromised. It's fundamental to first establish the CX relationship to primary business KPIs. Key behavioural drivers, similar to recommendation or satisfaction are not the outcome the business measures success against. They are indicators of outcome. The closer the correlation of the indicator to the outcome, the more reliable and therefore important it is in CX.

Sadly, there isn't a single indicator you can rely upon to

inform enough of the business outcome alone. There are in fact 300 behavioural drivers[1] which customers (as humans) subconsciously select from depending on the decision to be made.

By identifying the most important of these combined indicators, you can provide an almost complete picture of what matters most to your customers. You then have an enviable business asset.

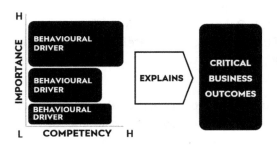

Figure 1. This diagram illustrates several key behavioural change drivers (what matters most). Each has a differing importance value to customers and is perceived to be delivered by the company to a greater or lesser degree of competence. The total of these explain how CX contributes to critical business outcomes.

Measuring behavioural change means you are measuring the indicators relevant to the desired critical business outcome. This allows the organisation to reliably act upon findings because the key behavioural drivers answer the question, 'what matters most to customers when it comes to achieving our critical business outcomes'.

How To Effectively Measure Behavioural Change

There are several approaches. Having worked with or studied various, I have found the award winning EXQ scale (Customer Experience Quality Measure) produced by Prof Dr Phil Klaus[2] the most reliable and actionable available.

EXQ is based on a refined list of 300 behavioural change drivers from which Prof Dr Phil Klaus identified 25 drivers account for 90% of customer decision making. Unlike other approaches, the importance of key behavioural drivers is defined by customers from each brand. Each brand's EXQ score and composition of key behavioural drivers differ. I express this as the brand's CX DNA.

The 25 drivers of EXQ are spread across three stages of customer relationship; pre-purchase (brand experience), purchase (service experience) and post purchase (post purchase experience). Below is a summary of Professor Dr Phil Klaus drivers. Full descriptions of statements used in the analysis are available[3].

- Pre-purchase Brand Experience – Brand importance, expertise, independent advice, true costs, importance of service personnel, value perception (product), value perception (competitors)

- Purchase/ Service Experience – hand holding support, process ease, transparency, flexibility, omni-channel consistency, interpersonal skills, customer service personal relationship, services design, efficient design

- Post purchase Experience – convenience, familiarity, proactivity, relationship versus transaction, service recovery, emotional reward, social approval

Arriving At An EXQ Score

A short qualitative phase is conducted to ensure the question statements are understood by customers. This is followed by quantified research to 125 customers per study. Customers are asked to value each statement between 'very important' through to 'not important at all'. They are also asked to declare share of category by brand and provide examples of where the statement is delivered.

This provides a ranking of key behavioural drivers, prioritised by the most valuable to the most important customers. A similar ranking is produced for your competitors. Comparing the leading key behavioural drivers informs whether they are distinctive to your brand or expectations of the sector.

Figure 2. Output from utilities EXQ study. Key behavioural drivers ranked by 'what matters most' in relationship. Each code represents a key behavioural driver statement e.g. SP5 'I always deal with the same person/process at XYZ', BRE2 'I am confident in XYZ's expertise' or PPE3 'XYZ keep me up to date'.

In this example, we can see the first ten EXQ key behavioural drivers account for 2/3rd of customer decision making. Whereas the lowest scoring ten EXQ statements account for 10%. This highlights how important it is to be able to convert what matters most in action. If the same resource is applied to manage the customer experience for the two sets of key behavioural drivers, one would be six times more effective than the other.

The overall performance of the drivers is calculated to provide a score out of 100. Companies at the highest level expect a 600% return on their CX investment[4].

Applying The Findings
To Improve Your Customer Experience Success

Accountability makes key behavioural drivers analysis, and EXQ in particular, significantly more informative as a CX business tool. It provides many business profit increasing opportunities:

1. The business can invest resources, with confidence, more effectively and efficiently in activities deemed important to customers,

2. The more customer experiences the brand promise is aligned to key drivers, through the interactions encountered, the more inclined customers are to increase their share of category contribution,

3. You can look across the entire customer journey to see how often the key behavioural drivers occur and how well they are delivered to take action accordingly,

4. The verbatim feedback provided by customers for each key behavioural driver details their experiences. This enables the CX improvement team to pinpoint touchpoints for improvement sooner.

5. Distinction can be made between areas which customers value, but expect from all competitors, and those which they value but only associate with your brand. Ensuring marketing and propositions are effective,

6. Without key behavioural driver insight anything which performs badly is attended to and fixed, even if its not valued by customers. This creates unnecessary waste,

7. Once several key behavioural drivers are established, the most important can be tracked through Voice of the Customer programmes just like satisfaction or recommendation. This provides a more meaningful customer performance dashboard, which will be welcomed by senior managers,

8. With continuous feedback, individual negative customer feedback can be intervened. With a specific key driver associated to a negative score it is much easier for front line agents to identify the problem and resolve it sooner. A generic satisfaction of recommendation score is reliant on customer verbatim being included.

To organise how to apply the EXQ findings, I have developed the MILO matrix. Each key behavioural driver and the associated experience can be plotted. The matrix is based on two axis, 'what matters most' and 'how well it's delivered'. This provides four alternate actions to take with the study findings:

- **Manage** – Experience is poorly delivered, but also it's not important to customers. Recommendation is, unless a regulatory obligation, manage the activity out of the customer experience.

- **Improve** – Experience is poorly delivered, but considered important to customers. This is a priority. Without improvement business will be lost to the competition.

- **Leverage** – Experience is well delivered and it's important to customers. This is an opportunity for competitive advantage. It is a key reason customers choose you so it should feature heavily.

- **Opportunity** – Experience is well delivered, but it's not important to customers. The opportunity is to transfer this strength to an area of importance to customers. Continued focus in this area will distract you from what's really important and over time frustrate your customers.

Figure 3. MILO Matrix ©Clientship.

Key behavioural change drivers inform business priority outcomes. They provide a voice for the customer which can be presented in a business like way. This empowers you to challenge for investment, resource and prioritisation for customer experience improvements on a commercial basis. By doing so you also increase the respect for CX internally.

When improvements relating to drivers are implemented, the performance of the drivers will also increase. Customers will find it easier to choose your brand for the customer experiences that matter most to them. The customer performance dashboard will light up with the increase in key behavioural drivers. Overall, the value of your CX increases to your organisation.

Taking The Next Step To CX Success
With Key Behavioural Drivers

I have been working with Prof Dr Phil Klaus for many years. As one of the few trusted advisers of his work in the world, I have applied EXQ and this approach with many organisations. Through my company Clientship, we support clients to transform their customer experience programmes in this way to deliver a significantly more rewarding outcome.

We have several case studies demonstrating the strength and the return that can be achieved. These are available on request.

References

1. Klaus.P Customer Experience Quality Measures study identified c300 drivers account for c100% of decision making

2. Klaus.P (2015). *Measuring Customer Experience.* Palgrave Macmillan Publications

3. Klaus P Taken from the EXQ© scale with kind permission of Prof Dr Phil Klaus

4. Klaus.P (2015). *Measuring Customer Experience.* Palgrave Macmillan Publications

About Christopher Brooks

Christopher Brooks is Managing Director of International Customer Experience Practice Clientship. With a specialism in end to end customer-centric transformation programmes, the Clientship reach now extends to UK, Europe and South America with offices in Spain, UK and Mexico.

Steering Clientship, Christopher works with international corporates, shaping their customer strategies to increase sustainable growth from customer centricity. Christopher is also a regular contributor to the CX trade press running the popular CX Leaders series in MyCustomer, hosting the CXSuperheroes podcast show as well as guest lecturing at The International University of Monaco's PhD Luxury Management course. Christopher is a regular judge for customer marketing and experience effectiveness awards. Most recently he founded the global social cause initiative, the Customer Experience World Games.

https://clientship.com

christopher.brooks@clientship.com

Phone: 0044 7968316548

LinkedIn https://www.linkedin.com/in/christopher-brooks-1425b7a

twitter https://twitter.com/consultingchris

Fast Track Your CX Plans With A Rating Metric

Hannah Foley

Have you ever wondered how some new start-ups get off the ground so fast? Some of the best products or services struggle to see the light of day whilst others, which in comparison may be incredibly similar, fly off the shelves. Today's consumer has started to reduce the number of sources they trust for recommendations. At the same time attempting to build confidence in more of their buying decisions - not simply higher value or emotional purchases such as holidays or cars. Consumers (b2b & b2c) need proof that they are making the right decision and they don't want to wait to find it. They crave digital proof at their fingertips. As a consequence, with the right strategy you can build customer trust and grow, faster.

This is what I'm talking about....'Consumer review websites now rank 2nd most trusted by consumers in the UK and US to provide honest opinion about a good or service. Only 'family and friends' rank higher.'

Open review platforms are experiencing major growth in UK, Europe & Americas. Nine out of the top ten UK startups from 2019 are actively using an open review platform (predominantly Trustpilot) and at least 75% of them are actively gathering and promoting ratings on their website.

Rank	Company	Sector	Platform	No. of reviews	Inviting reviews	Responding to reviews	Rating on website	Current score
1	Revolut	Finance	Trustpilot	64k	Unclear	Yes - to the bad ones	No	4.5
2	Igloo	Energy	Trustpilot	1k	Yes	Yes - to the bad ones	Yes	4.6
3	Trouva	Retail	Reviews.io & Trustpilot	4k	Yes	Yes - bad & some good	Yes	4.6
4	Soldo	Finance	Trustpilot	>750	Yes	Yes - All	Yes	4.3
5	Elder	Healthcare	Trustpilot	>450	Unclear	Yes - All	Yes	4.4
6	Glenhawk	Finance	None	-	-	-	-	-
7	Zego	Finance	Trustpilot	1.3k	Yes	No	Yes	4.6
8	Streetbees	Tech	Trustpilot / Google Reviews	50+	No	No	No	Various
9	Guestready	Hospitality/travel	Trustpilot	>500	Unclear	Yes	Yes	4.6
10	Thriva	Tech	Trustpilot	>750	Yes	Yes - to the bad ones	Yes	4.6

So, what has this got to do with Customer Experience Measurement, Metrics & ROI? The use of open review platforms gives your business a very transparent customer driven metric. This metric could be used to accelerate your businesses adoption of a customer experience strategy. Here are five key benefits to gathering reviews accompanied by some examples of how to use your review platform adoption to land other recommended strands of a good CX strategy.

Five CX Benefits Of Gathering Open Ratings

1. Purpose built review platforms take process pain out of managing customer feedback. You are buying into an off-the-shelf platform which is built on today's consumer need to share their experiences and connect with the brand and to benefit others who are earlier in their buying decision.

2. The platforms have created a common rating language which is simple to understand, a customer driven metric from which to galvanise teams and leadership around. Everyone can access the rating, anytime.

3. Furthermore, because the ratings and the accompanying reviews are highly visible it naturally drives action and better behaviours. No (good) employee wants to see their name attributed to a poor review and when the great reviews come in, they can see the contribution they made to improving the rating.

4. The platform widgets have made it easy to use the ratings for on-site promotion, contributing to reduced bounce rates and increases in conversions.

5. So, arguably maybe the best benefit of all for accelerating your CX strategy, is that these ratings can easily be attributed to revenue and profitability overcoming our challenges with securing VOC investment.

Whether you are a start-up or working with a more established company, bringing your teams together around a customer score is fundamental. A transparent score shifts you up a gear and will help to fast forward your CX activities, but it's important you lead a well thought through implementation. Here are some pointers and examples of the four pillars you may want to consider for your implementation. If you're already using open review platforms you may find this content helpful to maximise its effectiveness for your organisation.

Pillar One - Colleagues

How will you respond to reviews? Do you need a dedicated resource or can this add a fresh dimension to someone in the customer service team's role? You could develop new career pathways into the CX department.

Finding people to own and manage closing the loop ensures that your business and customers have better outcomes.

Reward and recognition linked to the reviews works exceptionally well with these platforms. I've seen dedicated screens in customer service departments with new reviews appearing live, and in smaller companies every employee getting an email when a new review is left, from frontline staff to the board. Imagine the buzz you'd have as a member of the customer services team when the MD walks by and gives you a high five for the glowing review 'Dawn from Scunthorpe' just left mentioning how brilliant you were.

Peer to peer coaching – when a pattern of five-star reviews emerges for particular team members why not enlist them to be your CX champions or share their customer stories. Using the insights you glean from the platform reviews, it is easy to identify the people within your organisation whose customer focus could help others to improve.

Pillar Two - Brand

Set the tone - start your implementation with a low volume pilot by inviting a test segment of your customers to leave reviews. Build a collaboration between your CX team, brand team and customer service team to respond to reviews, test responses and learn from them. Find authentic ways to communicate your brand voice and customer empathy or appreciation. Future customers don't just judge you on the reviews, they judge you on the way you respond to reviews. Demonstrate how much you care.

Flaunt those reviews – you don't need to be at five stars to be shouting them from the rooftops, in actual fact many consumers are dubious if you are 'perfect'. Get those scores on your website homepage, flaunt them on your social media channels, pop them on your email signatures. Use the reviews to show that it's not just you they have to believe but '1,800 customers reviewed us and said we are 4.6/5 stars'.

Don't fear a few bad reviews, if future customers can see that when something doesn't go to plan you can be trusted to listen and make it right – you'll be quids in.

Pillar Three - Customer

Responding to negative reviews - Responding well to negative reviews can have a longer-term positive impact. According to a study by Trustpilot of consumers in UK, Europe and North America:

'When customers feel their reviews have been responded to appropriately, more than half admitted to shopping at the same location again. More than 2 in 5 customers would even go so far as to reverse their overall rating of the company and edit their review into a more positive critique. For 25% of people, how well companies respond to criticism can even help transition them from detractors to overall promoters of that company.'

Therefore - always thank the customer for their comment, explain what you are going to do now or why you can't do anything about it (there may be a very valid reason like a regulatory restriction etc) and be authentic. When you have addressed the problem – why not ask the customer to change their score and leave a review based upon the outcome?

Making experiences better – with clear visibility of things that make a positive difference to your customer and what frustrates them. Utilise site insights to prioritise improvements then strive to find a method that enables your business to act on feedback trends as they emerge. Are there obvious themes in your sub-three-star ratings? Find things to fix and fix them; observe the uplift in your rating as you reduce the low score reviews. One financial service organisation I worked with had a 'CX magic wand' linked to their Trustpilot scores – when they spotted a poor experience theme emerging in the reviews they 'waved their wand' and colleagues had to prioritise fixing the issue. It highlighted to everyone that customer satisfaction mattered and when something caused customers (and subsequently frontline colleagues) significant pain it was a priority. The service recovery response was swift and reassured customers that their time reviewing was well spent - *'we listened and acted'.*

Some of the leading platforms have also developed their text and sentiment analytics capability to help identify those emerging themes – to build customer journey, product, service and proposition improvements or even innovations.

Leaving reviews to help others – contrary to popular belief most companies have many more positive reviews than negative ones. If your customer takes their time to leave a review to help other future customers choose your business, you should design in the capability to thank them for their efforts. Loyal customers are incredibly valuable and ones that want to actively endorse you – they should be put on a 'top customer pedestal'. Imagine what they are worth in marketing budget if consumers trust reviews more than they do your actual advertising?

Pillar Four - Leadership

Customer feedback at their fingertips – ensure your leaders are on the pulse of the business by having real-time access to customer feedback. Get it in their faces so they see issues or brilliance as it happens - that's how you'll get buy-in to make things better.

Most review platforms aren't free, or the enhanced capability isn't, so you'll need to build a business case as you would any VOC investment. After a pilot or identification of similar case study you should be able to model and set expectations. Some of which could be short term and not require 12 months of historical data modelling – you will be able to see immediate impact (with the right implementation) on website bounce rates, social media click throughs, customer acquisition, satisfaction & retention metrics.

Shareholder or investor belief – build your business credibility by being transparent and open with your customer feedback in real time. If your chosen platform contributes to Google Seller Ratings, then you will get search engine optimisation (SEO) benefits and your ratings will be digitally more visible.

So that's it! If you've struggled to find a customer metric that everyone can rally around, then hopefully this has given you some food for thought. Rating platforms aren't all built on the same basis and it will be crucial to assess which one is best for your customer. There's no doubt that with a great implementation 2020's customer will be happy to leave a review. You will 'out' the great, the good, and the ugly of your customer's experiences, expeditiously show how CX efforts impact the bottom line and if your leadership won't back that ... you'll realise they aren't as serious about the customer as you are.

References

1. The critical role of reviews in Internet trust, 2020 – CANVAS8

2. The Startups 100 2019: the UK's best and most exciting new businesses revealed - https://startups.co.uk/startups-100/2019/startups-100-2019/

3. Bad reviews: why people write them, and what they expect, Published 6 September 2018, https://uk.business.trustpilot.com/guides-reports/learn-from-customers/bad-reviews-why-people-write-them-and-what-they-expect - Trustpilot

About Hannah Foley

Hannah Foley is a customer experience consultant and avid trekker. She has spent 15 years working for FTSE 100 B2B construction & financial services organisations as well as trekking to Everest Base Camp in 2012.

Hannah is a CCXP, NPS Certified practitioner, UKCX Awards Finalist 2017, UK CX Awards Judge 2019 and B2B specialist.

In 2019 she founded 'Yak' a UK based CX consultancy with a mission to help businesses get off on the right CX foot to #bemoreyak – consistent, able to weather the storm, high performing and well respected in their customer centric approach.

To connect with Hannah follow her lively & honest social content on:

https://www.linkedin.com/in/hannah-foley/

Instagram @yakcx

Twitter @cx_yak

www.yak-cx.co.uk

Is Net Promoter Score
The Magic Number For Your Business?

Umer Asif

If we were to ask ten different organisations what Customer Experience (CX) metrics they use, it would not come as a surprise that Net Promoter Score (NPS) features in most, if not all, of their CX dashboards. If we then ask them to explain how NPS has helped them drive dollar value and growth in their business, I can bet most of them may not be able to provide a convincing answer.

Since the creation of NPS by Fred Reichheld in year 2003, the metric has become the most popular CX measure for any industry. Companies have made claims of being better in customer experience delivery, based on this number, while some have made relentless efforts to become the best in class. NPS benchmark studies and consultants on the other hand have done good business.

It is not possible to examine NPS in just one chapter or provide numerical evidence for my views. However, as a CX practitioner, I have used NPS for over ten years, researched into its merits and demerits and listened to numerous expert opinions about it. I will explain in simple words what NPS really tells you, and help you decide if it is a number your organisation should run after.

What Is Net Promoter Score?

I am sure most of you already know what Net Promoter Score or NPS is. However, to examine the metric, it is important to revisit what it is.

NPS was introduced by Reichheld in 2003 in his Harvard Business Review Article "One Number You Need to Grow" and later led to his book titled "The Ultimate Question – Driving Good Profits and True Growth". Reichheld was researching a single metric that could allow businesses to determine the current state of loyalty without lengthy customer surveys. Based on this research and the correlations drawn, NPS was developed as an indicator for loyalty and growth for businesses.

NPS is most often based on a zero to ten scale. I have seen scales of five points, though it is debatable if they really give you the true NPS score. The question asked to the customer is, *How likely is it that you would recommend [this brand/product/service] to a friend or colleague?* – usually after a certain purchase, service, or brand interaction.

Customers who answer 9 and 10 are called *Promoters*; between 7 and 8 are *Passives*; and 6 or under are *Detractors*.

Net Promoter Score (NPS) = % Promoters - % Detractors

Once a statistically relevant number of responses are collected, the percentage of Promoters and Detractors are calculated. As an example, if 100 people responded of which 30 were Promoters, 60 were Passives and 10 were Detractors, then the Promoter percentage would be 30% and Detractor percentage would be 10%. Subtracting the percentage of Detractors from the percentage of Promoters gives us the Net Promoter Score, which in this case would be 20.

Theoretically, the NPS can range from a low of -100 (if every customer is a Detractor) to a high of 100 (if every customer is a Promoter).

There are certain behavioural differences between Promoters, Detractors and Passives. Promoters are considered more loyal and less price-sensitive because they believe they are getting good value overall from the company. They buy more, more frequently, compared to Detractors, and talk more positively about their experiences. Detractors on the other hand switch to other brands at a higher rate and will speak more negatively about their experience. Passives are the less vocal type, who do not have much loyalty for the brand. They may not be unhappy but are not loyal enough to stay if compelled by better competitive offers. The objective of every organisation should be to retain its current Promoters, convert Passives to Promoters and either convert the Detractors by addressing their concerns or completely lose them, to prevent more harm.

Reading through the above may make it sound like NPS is a simple metric, however, you would be surprised how many people who frequently use the number, may not fully understand what it is or how it is calculated. It is a good idea to keep reminding your stakeholders how NPS is derived and what the underlying percentages means for your business.

NPS, Merits And Demerits

If you scour the internet, you will find an equal number of Promoters and Detractors for the NPS itself! What is good about NPS is its simplicity and popularity as a CX metric. It is more popular than other metrics like OSAT (Overall Satisfaction) or CSAT (Customer Satisfaction), something that everyone talks about and benchmarks against. It is also a valid indicator of the level of satisfaction, as unhappy customers logically would not recommend a company, so a correlation between customer satisfaction and NPS does exist.

Where NPS raises questions and controversy is its design intent as a measure of loyalty and growth. The premise itself is based on whether you would recommend the company or experience to friends or colleagues. How many people who, on a feedback survey, say they would promote your company or service, actually do that later? How would you know if those recommendations converted into profitable new customers? Experience shows that customers are more likely to spontaneously share their negative experiences, on channels like social media, than positive ones, unless the positive experience was exceptional (or they are some social media influencers!). That is why, for your Voice of Customer programs, you need to keep inviting customers to share feedback, without which you would not get as many responses, or get more extreme feedback on both ends of the scale. Online retailers like Amazon or Etsy actively invite you to share your experience rather than asking if you would recommend your purchase to others and then leave it at that. It is only when a customer actively shares their views, that they could be positively or negatively influencing a purchase decision.

Another big limitation of NPS is the assumption that the scoring scale and methodology is universally applicable. Having led global CX programs, I know that culturally and generationally how you score on a scale varies a lot. The metric was developed seventeen years ago in an era when none of the social media platforms existed. A Detractor was not a thumbs down or a Promoter a smiling emoji. Every customer did not have a phone camera in their pocket. A single social media post could not make or break businesses or start a revolution. Artificial Intelligence was not a buzz word and customers did not voluntarily provide millions of data points about their daily lives for free. The NPS research was based on a certain set of businesses and industries, which too have greatly changed and evolved over the years.

In this reality, still assuming that Detractors are six points on a scale, without a clear understanding of what sets apart a Detractor rating six from someone rating zero, is just skimming the surface without delving into the problem and insights. I am sure some of you must have come across a service agent who has invited you to fill a survey and specifically suggested you give a nine or ten for the NPS question, as if their life depended on it. A customer rating seven or eight is likely happy and in many cultures, could be loyal, but this segment is not even considered in the determination of this metric.

There are several studies that have been conducted, that do challenge the over simplistic assumptions of NPS. Given how sharing feedback and experiences has changed, it would make sense to revisit and validate the NPS scale to see if it is still relevant to the current time and as value adding as it seemed, back when it was launched.

Net Promoter System

While I am sceptical about the Net Promoter Score as a metric, I am more agreeable to Reichheld's views in his second book on the topic, 'The Ultimate Question 2.0'. Recognising some of the limitations of NPS, Fred talks about creating a Net Promoter System, rather than just focusing on the number. He acknowledges some of the limitations of the scale, the way the questions could be asked and how value is associated to the Promoters, Passives and Detractors. He states that 'NPS is a business philosophy, a system of operational practices and a leadership commitment, not just another way to measure satisfaction'and that NPS is a flexible and open source system that organisations can adapt to their needs, while maintaining some fundamental requirements. In this book, a lot of importance is put on the constituents of the NPS rather than the score and the importance of how leadership drives the culture around it.

I believe if an organisation really wants to have NPS as a key metric, then they need to understand and adopt the full philosophy and stop comparing themselves against external benchmarks.

More important than the NPS score is understanding the Detractors, Promoters and Passives, and looking into the insights to see what is driving these opinions. But even before getting into that, they should do their own internal exercise to determine if they see a correlation of their customer behaviour to the original NPS scale, or whether it would be better to adapt the scale for their business. Another fundamental question to ask is, what is the right question to ask for their business? Is likelihood to recommend bringing more value or does it make more sense to ask if they are likely to return? Would asking about likelihood to, say, renew a membership help gain more loyalty (and value) than asking if customers would recommend the membership to others? Once you have answered these questions, you may determine that NPS is not the right metric for you. Or if you determine it is, then understanding the value of each underlying component and driving a clear understanding of it from top leadership, down to the frontline, and taking actions to convert Detractors, would bring more value than chasing the absolute number.

If Not NPS, What Else?

There are various other options out there for alternatives to NPS. Metrics like Customer Effort Score (CES), which determine how much effort a customer had to make to get an issue resolved, are measured later in the customer journey and help assess things like customer churn. You could even come up with your own metric for something that may be very important for your customers.

However, in my experience, if you really want to understand what is impacting your customer loyalty or driving value, the answer most probably already lies in the mounds of customer data that you may already be collecting as part of your loyalty or customer experience measurement programs. Having a simpler metric for satisfaction like CSAT, making more effort trying to determine what is driving the satisfaction, correlating it with value and then actually doing something about the insights, will produce much better results. If you already have a loyalty program or collect customer data through other interactions, then do more data mining and correlations using that. Millennials and Gen Z like to share everything online. Investing more in your social listening and data mining tools, within data privacy regulations, is ever so important. Investing in these capabilities compared to traditional NPS surveys, will bring more insights, and returns.

I may not have given you a definite recommendation, but I hope I have given you some food for thought to make you think about how much weightage you want to give NPS on your CX or loyalty dashboard.

To sum it up, go for what is most impactful for your business and not what may be more popular!

About Umer Asif

Umer Asif is a Forrester Certified Customer Experience professional with over thirteen years of experience designing and implementing sales performance and CX programs. He works for a global energy company, leading CX measurement and innovation programs impacting over seventy countries.

Umer's forte is CX measurement. He has hands-on experience developing mystery shopping, Voice of Customer, Voice of Employee, and brand assessment programs.

He has also expertise in performance and reward management of frontline employees and integrating CX delivery with frontline performance.

CX is a passion for Umer. He loves to share knowledge, connect with other CX professionals, and help others improve. He has been a Judge at various international CX Awards over the last few years. Umer is also a CXPA Calgary Network Leader and currently working on developing a global CXPA community of CX professionals in multinational organisations.

To connect with Umer, reach out to him via LinkedIn at

linkedin.com/in/umerasif

Or visit his website at

umerasif.com

6. CX Strategy

Alignment, Communication and Direction

David Vs Goliath:
How To Attain And Maintain
A Competitive Advantage

Sarb Rana

When I started my first business, I had a fear that my competition, who were established businesses, with almost endless resource, would beat me. Whilst this can be true in some cases, I realised that they will not be able to copy what differentiates me from them. In my story I want to share with you how I used this approach to not only challenge, but also beat my established competitors.

What Was My Inspiration?

My CX journey started soon after leaving university working part time in a family business. Having studied some modules focussed around brands and customer journey's I had a good grasp of this subject but would not regard myself as an expert. That is why it was more surprising for me to notice the shortcomings surrounding the customers, be it blatant or out of ignorance. The first thing that struck me was the absence of the customer in the whole process. The only two interactions that occurred were when the customer placed an order and when they had to pay. There was no dialogue, breaking the ice questions (weather, sport, pets etc) or upselling! Which is very unusual in a face to face retail environment.

Despite this, of an evening customers would be queuing out the door waiting attentively to get their food for later that evening.

What got me thinking was two things; firstly what an amazing business this would be if only more focus was given to customers and secondly the food must be amazing for customers to keep on returning while being treated in a manner no sane person would accept in today's day and age. This is where my entrepreneur journey started, and at the centre of it all building meaningful customer relationships.

With a burning desire to be my own boss and knowing a little about the fast food industry I set out with a vision, of what I wanted my customers to experience, and no money to make it happen! I borrowed off family, got a bank loan and met an amazing bank manager along the way who helped and guided me to purchase my first ever fast food premises.

Living The Dream

Fast forward a few months and I was now the owner of a closed former fast food premises which clearly found it difficult to compete with the local competition, and I could see the family business I worked in going in the same direction. I remember sitting in the customer seating area on my own for what seemed hours questioning whether I had made the right decision. We were sandwiched between McDonalds, KFC, Subway and Pizza Hut. In the early days we had a lot of negative opinions from passers-by, family members and our first few customers all of them wondering whether we would last the Winter. Failure was not an option and I just had to believe in putting the customer first and building those relationships.

I saw those individuals as potential customers and treated what they were telling us as feedback. I tried to understand what lay behind there prophecy that we were doomed to fail. It was all grounded in the fact we were surrounded by competitors that were larger than us, could sell a similar product cheaper than us and had deeper pockets than us. Basically, they could do whatever we were doing without breaking a sweat. The quintessential David Vs Goliath.

Figuring Out The Solution

So for weeks on end I spent anytime I could spare analysing each of those competitors from product offerings, customer journeys, branding etc How could we stand out from the noise and make ourselves heard while adding value to our customers on a shoestring budget. I had analysed our competitors but one thing I had not done was analyse ourselves. One of the things business owners spend too much resource on is focussing on competition and trying to be more like them. Instead of looking internally and saying, 'what can I do differently'. We had made an excellent start, steady footfall, returning customers, branding on point, hired some excellent loyal front of house staff who hit the ground running (with little direction from an inexperienced first-time business owner). We had a good base to build from albeit a low one.

I was always a numbers kind of guy and into the detail so I began measuring our footfall, broken down into days, hours, minutes. As weeks went on, I noticed the same customers purchasing the same food items on the same day at near enough the same time week in week out. You could synchronise them against a Swiss watch. It was a habit which we had to take advantage of somehow, in a way which would be difficult to replicate.

Relationships Are Better Than Transactions

During my analysis of our competitors I noted the number of staff that worked there. How many times have you been to a national chain of any food restaurant and been served by the same person more than once? Rarely I hear you say. And that's when I realised that to make meaningful relationships you need time and in this context the only way you were going to get that was if you were served by the same person week in week out. We changed all our staff rotas to make sure a customer would be served by the same customer service staff on their visit. The results were amazing! After about the third or fourth week not only were we on first names terms but it was common for me to eaves drop in on a conversations about pets, family bereavements, births, holiday destinations, issues with work colleagues etc We had become more than just another food establishment we were creating meaningful customer relationships. Something that was difficult to replicate and a point that was conceded by the director of one of the company's mentioned above.

All of this gradually translated through to higher sales figures, increased average spends of our existing customers, customer recommendations and the holy grail of business - brand ambassadors. (Although at the time I didn't know what they were). All smaller businesses regardless of what sector you are in grapple with the same fundamental problems and one of them being competition. To succeed you need to be creative with your solutions use out of the box thinking and be ingenuitive. Play to the strengths of being a smaller business such as authenticity and being genuine. No one will or can care about your business more than you and this will, when you have conversations with customers shine through. Brands spend millions of $ trying to portray this and you can do it for free!

Applying The Real Life Lessons

Smaller businesses have competitive advantages in abundance. For me one of the most frequently used was the ability to make and implement business critical decisions very quickly. Such as introducing new products instantly, discontinuing ones that didn't work, pricing decisions etc. And that is because you are a lean machine with flat management structures. Larger competitors ideas get caught up in their bureaucracy eventually they'll be able to copy you but turning around an oil tanker takes some time and when that time comes you will have moved on to something new or consolidated your position. One of the ways we did this was to change our product offerings every two weeks by introducing new flavours, we kept the ones customers liked and jettisoned the ones they did not.

A taboo subject for many smaller business owners is customer complaints, owners try to avoid them expecting them to resolve themselves. I on the other hand quite enjoyed listening to complaints because I wanted to understand more intimately what a customer expected and how they felt they had been let down. I saw it as an opportunity to improve our products and service, and so should you. The more successful you become the more complaints you will have so have system for dealing with them. Mine was simple:

1. Allow the customer to truly express themselves

2. Ask them what they feel will rectify the issue and if reasonable entertain it

3. Learn from the experience and the likelihood of them coming back will be quite high.

I think we almost became a victim of our own success. We held ourselves to such high standards from food quality to customer service that when something was even off slightly, they felt let down. (And rightly so) But that is a good thing you need to set the bar high because that is also the same metric your competitors will be judged by. So, if your customer does try out your competitor's product, I can almost guarantee they'll be back if you don't compromise on those standards.

I hope you are able to implement the three lessons I discovered, 1. Be agile 2. Complaints are your friend 3. Maintain high standards. I have since sold my fast food business, one that we expanded across the UK and am now involved with a financial start-up. The practical lessons I have shared with you remain at the forefront of my mind and I am implementing them now in a different sector but trying to achieve the same outcome. Think outside the box, try as many different approaches as you can and don't be afraid to make mistakes.

Oh, and I just want to remind you in the end David won.

About Sarb Rana BSc, CeMAP

Sarb Rana is a serial entrepreneur having founded companies spanning a breadth of sectors from FMCG to financial services. His journey began soon after leaving university and was destined for a career in investment banking but decided to become his own boss, a path he has not looked back upon.

He expanded his first retail business to multiple sites across the UK and exited after being bought out by a larger rival. He has moved on to become the CEO of a financial technology company looking to leverage his discoveries from earlier businesses.

His contribution in this book highlights strategies he has implemented successfully being a small business owner in a very crowded marketplace. And details how playing to small business strengths can help you be heard and identify the Achilles heel of bigger brands.

Contact Details

Links https://www.linkedin.com/in/sarb-rana-1a9bb8124

Launch An 'Out-Of-This-World' CX Strategy

Sharon Boyd

A phenomenal customer experience is a key business differentiator. There is little argument to be had here – so read on for a 'spaced-up' approach into creating and landing an out-of-this-world Customer Experience Strategy. In true geek-girl style, I've pinched a few space titbits from the launch of the Falcon 9 rocket – a joint venture between NASA and SpaceX from Summer 2020.

Just like launching a rocket into an intergalactic realm; companies need a clear vision and plan of how they will deliver their CX. To include:

- The end destination

- The course

- The speed

- The timing

- The passengers

- The objectives and success factors

- The RoI

- The milestones and risks along the way

- The communication plan

With NASA – even a tiny bit of peach-like fuzz around the plan will cost lives. With a CX strategy – it will cost customers. Which ultimately could cost you your livelihood/reputation/full head of hair.

Pre-Flight Checks

You need to ensure the right crew is assembled, all on the same page and suited up before you start. In the case of this particular launch – NASA and SpaceX (and all their third parties) joined forces. As is often the way in business, this collaboration pooled resources and expertise but also created complexity, so take your time if you are in a similar position. The launch was a success as the two companies had a united vision, strong buy-in, pride and discipline in their delivery.

Leadership and accountability for the mission are key, so ensure the right person is steering it from above. This person must be in touch with the operation and ultimately, the end customer. Space exploration is such an important aspect of America's strategy, that the Vice President is Chair of the National Space Council.

Ensure when building your strategy, you give thought to what success looks like. NASA and SpaceX have the 'luxury' of strictly programmed co-ordinates for their destination and milestones. We don't, so set your operation up carefully to collect the data and stories that will show success.

Don't be guilty of giving your rocket paintwork a touch-up, but not identifying the incoming asteroids.

Before you design your strategy, you need to have a firm idea of the obstacles your business and customer is facing. Whichever tools you use to do this, check that you are staying true to the issues in hand.

From personal experience, I have found that completing a Gemba walk with the full crew, is a fruitful way to ensure everyone understands the mission.

A Gemba walk is an opportunity to see your front-end operation first-hand, by observing your employees and the processes used to fulfil their duties. It highlights challenges that they face in delighting every customer in every interaction.

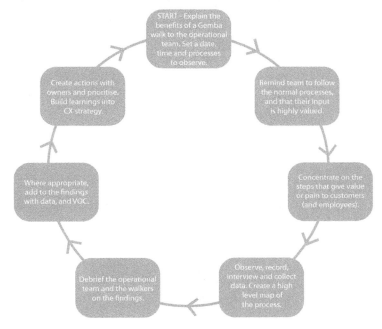

Gemba Walk Cycle by Canoodle CX

Employees frequently have fantastic ideas on how to switch up the customer experience that they offer, as well as pain points. They know what they need and as we know; employee experience can be a factor in the customer experience.

Employees will often also be customers of your business, and of your competition, meaning they can provide competitor insight too.

All of this data is a rich resource to build into your CX strategy.

Friction in silos is often the area causing most customer pain points. Test this – follow a customer 'baton' right from instigation to resolution and ensure any areas of friction are removed.

Just like the different departments in a business, a rocket is designed to be made up of different segments. These are separated by hatches, just like the barriers between each department, whether that is office politics, processes or locations. The hatches also facilitate docking to the International Space Station (ISS).

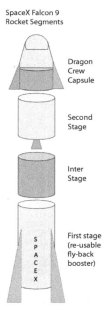

SpaceX Falcon 9
Rocket Segments

Dragon Crew Capsule

Second Stage

Inter Stage

First stage (re-usable fly-back booster)

Before the two astronauts could leave the crew capsule and enter the ISS; the pressure and temperature needed to be equalised between the two craft. In other words – they needed to be in alignment.

Importantly, ensure people are brought together across silos, and someone is solely accountable for the full end to end experience of your customer. Without accountability, your CX strategy will crash and burn.

3... 2... 1... Strategise

"Excellence is doing a common thing in an uncommon way."

Albert Einstein

Strategies are personal, they should be unique and strongly aligned to your brand, otherwise they just won't fly. Using an existing framework is no bad thing as a starter, but your teams, investors, and customers will spot it a lightyear away if there is a mismatch between your strategy, culture and brand. Whether you have a defined CX strategy or not, the way the business operates will already be out there, being felt in every interaction. Ultimately, the teams that deliver your strategy and the customers who see the fruits of it, must be able to recognise and connect it back to you.

Case Study

MKL are an Internet of Things (IoT) house in Yorkshire. The two founders are down to earth, fun, hands-on and very driven. Their mission is to deliver world-class tech and world-class CX. They have a very strong, upbeat and unique culture which is lived and breathed every day by the founders. A stuffy, fluffy or corporate-type strategy just would not hit the spot.

They leverage their stellar culture, ensuring their customers feel it positively with every interaction, and they always go the extra mile. Customers appreciate MKL's very authentic and straight-talking style. Together we created a CX strategy that matched them perfectly internally; and was also real to their customers.

A small section of the MKL strategy by Canoodle CX

Part of the MKL CX strategy would be delivered by the customer-facing engineers. Using complex business-speak and airy-fairy wording would be an instant turn-off. For this reason, the service behaviours that accompanied the CX strategy (and brought it to life) were written with the same tongue-in-cheek banter that the engineers use.

You won't find a strategy like MKL's anywhere else, the language used is completely tailored to them, and has landed perfectly. Importantly, the very unique strategy is published, externalised, and accessible for employees and customers alike; and is based on strong CX fundamentals.

Good CX strategies are the simple ones, but also don't scrimp on the finer details. For instance, the SpaceX team designed new, completely tailored spacesuits, with 3D printed helmets with a vision that they should look and feel just as amazing as a tux would. Tailoring is vital.

Be careful not to think that all of your customers are the same. That way you don't hit the requirements of any individual group, just somewhere in the middle. If you don't tailor to individual customer segment needs, your competitor will. Human centred design pays off when you come to the launch and embedding stages.

Building a CX strategy can be fraught. It can be easy to arrive in the 'zone of uncomfortable debate' – especially if you are challenging core values or stray into the failings of a department. If conflicts arise, refocus on the areas where you have compelling customer data or a clear impact on customer lifecycle value.

Good strategies always take several iterations and there are many routes to reach an end destination. As you design your strategy – don't discard the different options you've explored, as you may reconsider these further down the line. Retain a degree of built-in flexibility and plan this in to your timelines. SpaceX themselves had several issues before they were successful, so always expect some hiccups.

Taking key stakeholders along with you as you refine the strategy creates buy-in and ensures that no area of the business has been missed. Remember teams that are not directly customer facing i.e. legal or compliance departments can add huge constraints for your customer facing teams, if they are not onboard with your mission.

Exactly like NASA did, use Go/No Go check points to ensure everyone is ready before you launch your CX strategy. This might seem overkill – but each person giving the thumbs up is showing their commitment and a clear demarcation between the old world and the new.

But also don't wait until you have a 'go' before communicating your strategy. People need a heads up. Otherwise you may find yourself in a 'Houston, we have a problem' type scenario.

NASA runs comm checks to ensure the links to their remote teams (to outer space) are working. It is a good idea to test your channels and don't assume that comms have worked! Different people respond to different stimulants so be creative with your communication – especially as you land your CX strategy. When landing MKL's – we used a cartoon-style video and clever use of TikTok to share, which was absolutely on point for their brand.

Land And Be Prepared To Flex Your Strategy

Many companies spend months creating a perfect CX strategy, beautify it, and then stuff it in the proverbial drawer. Creation of a CX strategy cannot be a tick box exercise. Ensure it lands, just like SpaceX's Falcon 9 reusable rocket booster, which executed a perfect landing on a barge in the ocean. Seamless execution of a CX strategy, and the resulting value-add that you create for your customers, is where you win against your competitors. Though remember that what you perceive as value-add, and a customer's perception of value-add, may be wildly different – so always test your thinking with real customers. The success metrics you created upfront should evidence mutual success for the customer and your business, but do continue to ratify them.

The high-level strategic measures need to filter down to team and personal objectives. This will enable you to recognise and reward the right behaviours to deliver the CX strategy. Make it challenging for old behaviours to happen, preferably removing old processes completely.

Use customer stories to demonstrate the execution and impact of the strategy so that everyone can be clear on what it looks like. The acid test? Frame it through both a customer and employee viewpoint. In a world guided by the new strategy...

1. How would a customer describe their experience?

2. How would your employee describe the experience they are delivering?

Align these and you have the winning formula!

Like delivering any project or programme, the work doesn't stop once you've launched. Watch your CX strategy in action. Repeat your Gemba walks. Identify (and resolve) any new customer pain points. Check in with your front-line teams and of course your customers.

If 2020 has taught us anything, it's even the best laid plans can be knocked off course, so if needed, course correct – flex your strategy. However, by following the above steps, keeping a firm eye on your crew and your trajectory you'll be well on your way to delivering an out-of-this world CX strategy!

Over and out, Space Cowboys!

Sharon.

About Sharon Boyd

Sharon Boyd is MD of boutique consultancy Canoodle CX and Chief Customer Experience Officer (CXO) at MKL Innovation. She is also a qualified Programme Manager and Certified Customer Experience Professional. She was recently a non-exec director for over three years in the charity sector and is currently completing her Master's in Business Administration (MBA) at Cranfield University.

Sharon has over 20 years of experience in customer facing operations with technical knowledge, proven delivery and a strong customer focus. Having delivered multi-million-pound programmes for several large blue-chip companies across retail, hospitality, IT, telecoms and aviation, she brings a well-rounded approach.

She has created many strategies and visions for different organisations to successfully shape and drive the future of their business. Sharon is passionate about setting organisations up with the skills to deliver success. She is also ever so slightly – a self-professed geek-girl.

www.canoodlecx.com

Hello@canoodlecx.com

https://mkl-cx.webnode.com

https://www.linkedin.com/in/boydlsharon

Twitter and Instagram @CanoodleCX

Customer Experience Recovery: Why Planning For Failure Will Help You To Succeed

Katie Stabler

Have you ever experienced a truly terrible customer experience? Worse yet, felt like the offending organisation simply didn't seem to care? If your answer is yes, the likelihood is that you didn't remain their customer for long!

But what if they could have turned it around? What if they could have flipped your rubbish experience into an EPIC experience?

You would probably give them a second chance, right? Despite the problem you first encountered, their ability to recover your experience and leave you in an even better position than before would likely make you feel so impressed by their service that of course, you would stick around!

And that is exactly why customer experience recovery is so important, because no matter how amazing your organisation is, things go wrong.

So let's wind it back for a moment, what exactly is customer experience recovery?

It's the ability to proactively remedy a situation, turning bad customer experience into GREAT customer experience and making sure your customer swiftly moves from feeling dissatisfied to feeling that you have surpassed their expectations!

Customer Experience Recovery In Practice

So you know what customer experience recovery is, let me take a moment here to give you a couple of examples of customer experience recovery in action!

I'll start with my own professional experience, the pivotal point in my career where customer experience recovery started to become a true passion project. I was working in the world of finance (Debt Recovery to be precise), for an organisation where like many, the processes weren't perfect, employees made mistakes and external events impacted us and our customers. However, unlike most organisations, bad customer experience could have a significantly negative impact on our customer's circumstances and damage an already 'sensitive' relationship. As such, it was critical to develop a process which enabled us to quickly remedy a negative customer experience and fortunately, I was part of an excellent department which understood this need. Together we created a process which not only supported the proactive identification and customer-centric remedy of high impacting customer issues, it also supported a much needed cultural shift by bringing the leaders of multiple departments together to design solutions based around customer needs and wants.

But customer experience recovery comes in many forms and it doesn't have to be a complex process built to deal with extreme problems, it can come in more simplistic forms demonstrated by this next example.

This example comes from Ritz Carlton, world-renowned for epic customer experience and when I read this example quite some time ago, I couldn't help but smile and start sharing it with anyone who would listen...

Whilst Mrs Customer stayed at a Ritz Carlton resort she made a member of staff aware of a plumbing issue in her bathroom. She later dinned in the hotel restaurant, during which time a member of the service team promptly fixed the issue in her room. Mrs Customer returned to not only find the problem resolved but also to a personal note from the plumber with his name and number on, asking her to call him directly should the problem occur again and with it, was a little chocolate wrench.

This isn't rocket science but it is a brilliant example of how a personal touch and a little creativity can turn a negative experience into one which is guaranteed to make your customer smile.

Customer Experience Recovery: 3 Simple Steps For Implementation

So now you are comfortable with the concept of customer experience recovery and you've seen it in practice (I bet you can even think of a few personal examples?), let me walk you through three simple steps to help implement customer experience recovery.

Step 1. Plan For Failure

I am not a 'glass half empty' type person but when it comes to customer experience it is so important to recognise that no matter how much we care, no matter how much we plan, design and cultivate, sometimes things go wrong. Technology may let us down, people may fail us or we could be impacted by an external event completely out of our control and that is why you should have organisation-wide adoption of a customer experience recovery process. The process you design should:

- **Provide guidance on how to recover a poor experience:** Where possible, empower your team and allow them to react flexibly but give clear guidance

- **Let your team know what they are supported to do:** Be clear on what is and isn't possible, for example, if you have a compensation policy set clear levels of compensation permitted for each category of issue

- **Set expectations on how quickly you want the team to act:** Speed is critical, you should aim to proactively identify and remedy a bad experience before your customer has to take any of their own action

- **Support a collaborative approach across your organisation:** Don't work in silos. An issue that one customer experiences could be an issue many customers experience so work with your team to fully understand the situation

- **Promote an issue-tolerant culture:** A hidden problem isn't helpful to anyone, ensure your team are confident in raising issues without fear of repercussion

- **Close the loop:** Where appropriate, keep your customers informed. You might have only one or two customers that told you about the problem but you may have many more impacted so don't be afraid to hold your hands up, acknowledge the problem and proactively apologise, customers appreciate honesty and sincerity.

Step 2. Empower Employees

Your team are your best asset for amazing customer experience recovery! If they can quickly spot an issue, speedily remedy it, leave that customer feeling fantastic AND prevent a possible complaint then you have become the master of customer experience recovery.

Empower your team to become 'Recovery Heroes' by:

- **Providing them with clear guidance:** Detailed in step 1

- **Empower them to act on their authority:** With the right guidance and support your team should have the confidence to act quickly using their initiative

- **Support creativity and personalisation:** Where suitable, promote the use of creative customer experience recovery... Think back to the Ritz Carlton and their handy-man sweetening the situation with chocolate wrenches. Creative, personalised solutions will leave a lasting good impression.

Step 3. Fix The Issue!

You've done it. You've turned a rubbish experience into an epic experience and you now have a happy customer! But your work isn't quite finished yet, now comes the part where you do everything possible to prevent any other customer experiencing the same initial poor experience. Now is the time to:

- **Identify the root cause of the problem**

- **Understand its impact:** Is it a one-off or a repeating issue? Has it impacted the few or the many?

- **Work with your team to fix the problem:** Once again, collaboration is key. Work with the wider team to ensure the issue is fully identified and fixed

- **Throw in some additional quality assurance to ensure your 'fix' has worked:** Monitor that experience, map the journey your customers are taking to make sure the experience you intended is now the experience they are getting.

Customer Experience Recovery: Is It Worth It?

OK, so there's a bit of work involved and maybe you're thinking, "Why bother with customer experience recovery?" Well, you want to keep your customers right? If something goes wrong and your customer suffers, you surely want to fix it?

It's widely known that it is more profitable to retain an existing customer than to acquire a new one, and equally as important, loyal customers are more likely to be your best asset by telling all of their friends and family about you.

Another benefit not to be ignored is that organisations which excel at providing a great customer experience are more likely to have engaged employees, thus creating the much-coveted cycle of...

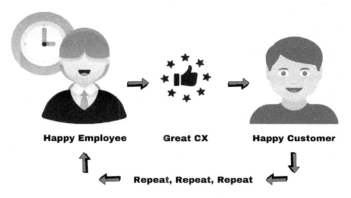

Happy Employee   **Great CX**   **Happy Customer**

Repeat, Repeat, Repeat

Also, consider the cost you could be avoiding. The cost of handling complaints (especially if you are a regulated industry), the cost of bad press, the cost of bad reviews, the cost of unhappy employees, the costs of issues identified too late. All of these costs can be mitigated by the use of effective customer experience recovery.

The bottom line is that customer experience recovery looks very different for every organisation but as long as you leave your customers feeling happy and satisfied despite any hiccups they faced, you are on the right track to great recovery, cost savings, brand enhancement and excellent customer retention.

About Katie Stabler

Katie is a customer experience specialist, dedicated to cultivating high-value customer experience through data, design and culture. Her work is driven by the principle "Make your bed, and then make their day!", meaning get the basics right and then create those 'wow' moments! She has spent over a decade in experience design for the most financially vulnerable customers working within both the not for profit and commercial sector and now is the Founder and Director of her own Customer Experience Consultancy.

Find out more about Katie and connect with her here:

https://www.cultivatecustomerexperience.com

https://www.linkedin.com/in/katie-stabler-ccxp-6475278a

https://www.instagram.com/customerexperience_provocateur

Would You Like To Contribute
To Future Editions of *Customer Experience?*

Customer experience as a professional is growing and evolving on a daily basis. There are many examples of innovative thinking and projects that have made a huge difference around the world.

The idea of this book is to allow CX practitioners around the world to share their stories for the mutual benefit of everyone. We are actively looking for new contributors for our next book which will be published in 2020.

Our first outing of *Customer Experience* has been a #1 international best-ranked, bestseller in the categories of *Customer Service, Customer Relations, Customer Experience Management, Consumer Behaviour* and *Marketing and Sales.* Clearly, professionals want to stay right up-to-date with what's happening in *Customer Experience Management (CXM).*

If you would like to get involved in the next release, then get in touch. All you need a good story to share that you know will add value to the readership.

If you would like the *Writer's Guide,* please email:

coachbiz@hotmail.com